"DEAR CHILDREN", A Manual for Adult Children of Divorce

25 Year Study of Spirituality and Overcoming the Effects of Divorce; Healing the World

Written by
William Hinckley

INSPIRED BY GOD

BALBOA.
PRESS
A DIVISION OF HAY HOUSE

WWW.DEARCHILDREN.INFO

Library of Congress Control Number: 2012909860

Balboa Press books may be ordered through booksellers or by contacting:

Balboa Press
A Division of Hay House
1663 Liberty Drive
Bloomington, IN 47403
www.balboapress.com
1-(877) 407-4847

ISBN: 978-1-4525-5316-0 (sc)
ISBN: 978-1-4525-5317-7 (hc)
ISBN: 978-1-4525-5315-3 (e)

Printed in the United States of America

Balboa Press rev. date: 11/12/2012

Dedication

To my leader, mentor and inspiration – God, who taught me about unconditional love, acceptance and inspired me to write this book. To my children, Chelsey, Evan, Benjamin and Rachel who gave me unbelievable joy as a father.

To my parents, who gave me my mortal body, and the opportunity to experience life.

To my God, who created this existence for my soul to be embodied and live a drama that could only be written by my Spiritual Father, to give my life meaning and happiness.

I hope to have only written things in this book that will produce high energy enough that it may elevate another human soul.

William

Contents

Preface

Dear Children, A Manual for Adult Children of Divorce is a practical guide to find meaning and happiness through a spiritual journey and to overcome the traumatic effects of divorce that often carry forward into adulthood. It is based on understanding the roots of childhood and how to follow a process to obtain spiritual peace through acceptance, forgiveness and finding true meaning in life. This book and its content can be read and applied by anyone seeking happiness and fulfillment in their personal life. It can also be used as a manual towards a better understanding of the challenges that someone may be facing as they deal with, or have attempted to deal with, the effects of divorce and separation. This is a story of my life and the effects that my divorcing parents had on me, but is not unlike many others who come to experience this earthly challenge of familial dysfunction. This book is not solely of my writing for the words have been placed on the pages through the inspiration of God himself. I was inspired to write this book and to ensure that it would be made available to others. While my experience may be somewhat different, each soul that enters this life is a gift from God – and has been empowered to fulfill their mission. This book is about that mission and what I have learned along the way. It is my hope that in reading this book you will find it informative, inspiring and applicable to assist you on your journey in this drama called life.

Introduction

Life is a wonderful expedition – but the wonder and joy is not always evident. With its many ups and downs, turns and loops, we are often left feeling empty inside and searching for a true purpose. We have many questions of life in every phase of our development. Even after many years of accomplishments, there are times we still ask ourselves if we have had a fulfilling life and whether or not the path that we have taken is the one that we are supposed to be on. We often look back with regret and disappointment and struggle to understand a meaning in life today.

Each individual that comes to this precious planet is unique in many ways. There may be times when we are mistaken for someone else that looks like us, but overall, each individual is distinct and not replicated in any other spiritual form. The closest means that we have come to replicating a human being is in the development of identical twins. Their DNA being an exact duplicate, produces an identical human form, however, the soul which is housed within the realm of each body is still unique and different from the other. Each individual has an exclusive character at birth and as each person goes through life experiencing a variety of social endeavors, the character of each person is further individualized by the events that occur.

Many times in life I have looked at my circumstances and questioned the purpose of my existence. I wondered why I had experienced one type of life as opposed to what my friend was experiencing or a complete stranger going through another set of circumstances. Often frustrated with my life and wishing to be living the life of another, I came to examine more closely - from a spiritual realm - the purpose for living. I began searching for the meaning of my life at a rather early age. I recall thinking to myself when I was 10 years old a scenario that was quite similar to the movie, "The Truman Show". I believed that I was in a world of actors that were put here on this planet to contribute to the growth and development of my life and future. No doubt this was a time in my life when egocentric thinking had become engaged - but I would return to this thought almost 40 years later and realize that this idea was not that far from the truth.

My life has been filled with many joys and sorrows that have allowed me to develop into the individual that I am today. These experiences are what makes us who we are and gives us the character that we have. Modern psychology has evolved to help individuals and society learn how to deal with human dysfunction that has been caused through traumatic events generally occurring in the early part of childhood. It seems that the earlier this trauma is experienced in a person's life, the more devastating the overall dysfunction and greater the challenge of dealing with correcting this at a later stage of life. My childhood was filled with the trauma of divorce which occurred in the mid 1960's. I grew up in a small rural farming community in which divorce was exceptionally rare and any understanding of the long term effects virtually unknown. It has not been until recent times that some of the effects – as well as strategies for dealing with the effects of divorce have become more widely understood. The research book written by Judith Wallerstein, *"The Unexpected Legacy of Divorce"*, is one such compilation of study. Ms. Wallerstien is a highly recognized child psychologist and has documented a study of children that she counseled from a very early age until adulthood. Her study looks at a comparison of children's lives that grew up in homes of trauma from marital discord. She looks at two study groups - one set of children whose parents had divorced and the effects on the children as the parent's continued to have ill communications or were undermining each other. The other study group consisted of families that had parents which were not happy, and often times experienced chronic arguing and discord in the family but remained in a married partnership where the children did not experience the separation of the parents. Ms. Wallerstein looks at the long term effects of how these two living conditions affect the adult relationship capabilities of the children that grew up in these homes. The research results indicate that the children who had parents that remained together, even with the presence of chronic discord, were much more successful in their own adult relationships as opposed to those children who suffered from the effects of parental separation.

"Dear Children" is a book that addresses the challenges of life as a result of my divorce experience. Marital separation is generally not amicable by any means, and often filled with conflict. In fact, the way in which parents deal with their relationship in most cases is unacceptable within the parameters of child psychology and social work. Even with the advancement of social sciences to assist families today, society and individuals still struggle with addressing the issues and needs of children who suffer from the effects of divorce - particularly at a very early age. For children of divorce, many of the dysfunctions they experienced in childhood are perpetuated within the realm of their own marriages and often to the eventual breakdown of the relationship. For the longest time, child analysts assumed the resilience of the child to adapt to virtually any situation that the custodial parent was deciding upon, would ensure the good standing of children. Such misguided thinking is built upon the idea that children can withstand whatever situation they may be placed in and emerge without any long-term damages or character-altering effects.

The divorce rate across North America has steadily climbed to 50% and higher for the past 30 years. I suspect the rate will continue to rise as a result of children being exposed to the effects of divorce. Some will have better conditions than others with respect to the child overcoming the unhealthy survival strategies developed in childhood but all will be affected. The intent of this book is to share knowledge towards an understanding of these effects and to correct the dysfunctions that developed as a result of the irreconcilable difference between the parents.

"Dear Children" is not only a book about gaining understanding, but it is also about hope and spirituality so that readers may find clarity in the meaning of life where meaning may not be completely evident. I will explain the path I took to come to an understanding and the complete healing that has given me great hope for the future and eternity to come. Knowing that my children also became victims of divorce, I was motivated to write this book in an attempt to explain to them what had happened in my life, and the understanding that had come to me as a result of my search. My hope is that with this understanding, they would be able to make corrections more quickly in their lives so that they would not suffer from multiple marriage failures and furthered broken homes to leave more children to suffer from this 21st century plague.

I credit this knowledge and the inspiration to write this book to a Spiritual Power, a Supreme Soul who created this great school called Earth and who has enlightened me through my own experience. He has given me purpose in sharing this knowledge with my children so that they may learn and benefit from my trials. This Powerful Being has directed me to put my story to paper and in the very least, benefit my children who are still in the early years of life. Even though divorce has affected the lives of these four children whom I love, my intent is to encourage them towards a different experience than the one that I had and possibly spare them at least some of the pain and agony by giving them the knowledge that I have come to know is true. For any others interested in learning from this experience, I hope you may benefit from whatever element of this story that speaks to you.

I have studied many different forms of religion and spirituality and have come to understand there is one God who manifests truth in many different venues. I have come to understand that there is truth in all religions and that the essence of goodness exists for all people to live by. All people and creations upon the earth share a common thread of elements which make up our physical beingness. According to the Hindu religion, all souls come to the earth and land on different branches or religions which fit the culture and geographic location in which we exist. Science has broken us down into water and elements from a periodic table which all matter on the earth shares and has some commonality to it. I believe one of our objectives in life is to understand how we are all the same and connected, rather than being apart and different. Whether people, plants and animals classify our species, or religion, culture, creed and race define our entity, we have the common essence of being at one with each other along with being one with God our creator. Our responsibility as parents is to ensure the sacredness of this understanding and to provide this oneness environment to our children.

I am an avid reader on books of spirituality. One source that has inspired me is a book written by Dr. Wayne Dyer called,

"The Power of Intention". Along with my Creator, I believe this book helped me find the courage and strength to believe in myself and to align my life with the power of Intention in order to assist me in accomplishing my objective of sharing this information. Dr. Dyer's book helped reaffirm the truth of God's existence and the spiritual essence of our mortality without being associated to any specific religion. It has also lent very practical knowledge of how we can experience being a part of Intention, or in other words, God's plan to co-create the world in which we live.

"Dear Children" is my personal memoir and what I have learned throughout life. I dedicate this book to my children and to the successes that they will experience in life as a result of a much greater understanding of our existence and ways in which to overcome the challenges of today. It is also a thank you to the many people and resources that have imparted knowledge that I might come to this eventual epiphany and to my least expected event of writing this book. It has been a privilege and joy to be able to create this book and share my words with others who may be suffering from the effects of being a child of divorce and the impact that it may be having on their personal lives and relationships. May we all heal from the devastating effects of such separation and grow to have improved relations and uplifting experiences that will give us the joy of living a full and complete life in a manner that God would want us to have.

Prologue

Before we begin this journey, I would first like to address a couple of issues. I would like to thank all of the people who have come into my life who have blessed me with knowledge, understanding and experience. There have been so many great teachers who have ultimately been actors in my drama and who have assisted me to learn and grow in truth. I take no credit for myself but give it all to God, my Creator and the author of my life story. He deserves complete praise for allowing me to share what has been compiled within the binding of this book. I quote from the scriptures, "Glory be to God in the Highest."

I would also like to acknowledge other outstanding individuals who have helped me progress towards a better understanding of the effects of divorce. There are many people who have recognized the importance of writing books and giving lectures on the topic of divorce and its effects upon children. Books have been written to assist parents to help their children to cope with the separation event both during and after its traumatic occurrence. There have also been a number of books written to help parents or adults deal with life during and after a divorce. Far fewer are the books available for adult children of divorce - those who have suffered the effects of such a detachment in their early years and are now trying to live as adults with all the inherent characteristics that were passed on to them as a legacy from their parents' unharmonious relationship. A knowledge base regarding the effects of divorce has evolved over time, however, there are generations of children from the 60's, 70's, 80's and 90's onward who have very little, if any, resources to help them with this traumatic occurrence and the lasting outcomes. Even today, with generations of evidence to say otherwise, society has somehow come to assume that the resilience of children will ensure they perceive the outcome of a break up in their home to be inconsequential. It is my hope that this information can serve to help get to the root of the problem and begin to heal the children who have had very little to say about the decisions their parents have made to drastically effect their lives in such a deleterious manner.

Laws have changed and policies legislated to address physical needs and care for children of divorce, but have only started to recognize the long term manifestations of the ill effects upon our society. It is sad to say that more visibly we have built bigger court houses, many more jails and certified thousands more clinicians to only band-aid the problem in our society. While I hope that this book will ultimately be for the healing of individuals who have went through divorce as a child, I also desire for government officials, professionals related to the social problem and the general populace as a whole to recognize that the only complete cure is to understand the significant and long term effects of divorce and to educate people regarding the weighty decision of marriage, and particularly in association with having children.

Realizing that as human beings, we will always make errors and that divorce will likely always exist. We need to recognize that the liberties the justice system has extended to individuals to divorce, should not impact the rights of children to grow up healthy with a stable, social, emotional and spiritual knowledge of their self worth and to not be deprived of their very basic and most essential need to feel love and regard by not only one custodial parent, but by two mature, competent and responsible individuals who are guided to work together for the benefit of the child. This is, in essence, what a marriage contract should be - in sickness and in health, for richer or poorer, for better or worse. The marital commitment and act of having children should not allow for some flimsy cop out where two parents go their separate ways just to satisfy their own selfish needs. At the point of having children, of bringing precious lives into this world, parents should be required to look beyond their own needs and to sacrifice for the needs of their children. We have established data that clearly documents that divorce has damaging and long term effects on children, and that a unified home provides a more solid and assuring base for children to at least have a greater chance of developing into healthy adults. In short, sacrificing for the sake of children and placing a higher priority on ensuring a family remains united and together is far more important than the individual desires that parents may have. We need to begin to understand how to reverse this great plague that has come upon our 21st century society in North America and around the world. When we can seriously look at eliminating the problem, we can stop attempting to remedy the problem with bandage solutions.

This book will begin to help us understand how to reduce this overwhelming society issue – by ensuring that more children grow up healthy and whole. We will also explore how children that have been damaged by the effects of divorce can be healed so that we again reduce the ever-growing concern of marital separation. We create healthy children by creating healthy families led by two biological parents that love and regard their children as a jewel that they value and that they wish to protect and never tarnish. Children, including adult children of divorce, can be healed through an education process that will help them recognize the characteristics that they developed to help them survive the devastation of a broken home. This insight and understanding will assist them to be aware of inherent traps that may cause future relationship problems, particularly the process by which they may select healthy life partners when considering starting their own relationships which may include children. While the details contained in this book were written directly from my experience as a child of divorce, I believe that many other types of dysfunction, including physical, emotional, sexual and other neglect and abandonment issues may be addressed with this information on the basis that the child of the dysfunctional home has suffered from a lack of love and regard. So let us begin the journey of understanding and healing, that even though the event was devastating, we can learn and grow to experience goodness from all of life and enjoy the drama that unfolds throughout this brief mortal existence.

Part 1:
Life in the Iron Age

Chapter 1: Life Before Birth

Dear Children,

When I was a child no one told me where I came from before I was born. Obviously, I didn't have the mental maturity at that age to comprehend even if someone would have taken the time to sit down and explain the concept of creation and the spiritual connection that we all have. While growing up, I heard a simple story about a stork that happened to drop off newborns from the sky. For such an important question of life, I think we do a rather poor job of understanding let alone explaining this to our children. I think in many ways, parents become desensitized to the whole miracle of birth from the sleepless nights and endless number of diaper changes – the insomnia and stress somehow makes them forget that this miraculous event could have only occurred through some act of faith.

Modern day science has advanced by untold leaps and bounds in our understanding of embryology, DNA, chromosomes and genetics, but while fascinating us with the process of cellular development and genetic trait determination, it has fallen short in defining the romance between the soul and the human body. With our enhanced understanding of neural connections and synaptic chemical transfer defining the cognitive process in the brain, we have almost come to convince ourselves that this human body is nothing more than certain elements from the periodic table and that it is self-operated rather than directed in life.

The reason I want to start talking about life before birth is because this is where we really all begin. Our life as a soul, an energy, an intention or life force - whatever you want to call it – our life began eternities before this planet earth ever existed. When I look out at the stars and the great expanse of the universe and galaxy, I am in awe of the astounding display of stars that we have identified and organized into constellations. Back when I was a child, the big excitement of the day was when the Apollo mission landed on the moon. It was a mind-blowing event – to have a man leave planet earth and walk on the surface of this circular orb suspended in space. And the immortalized words of Neil Armstrong, the American astronaut who took that first step and declared, "One small step for man, one giant leap for mankind". I remember so clearly watching this event on television as the astronauts stepped out of their capsule and actually walked on the surface of the moon. It was particularly revealing to see pictures of the Apollo space shuttle with the image of the earth in the background. Seeing pictures of the earth from the moon made a great impression on my life at that early age – and it would be a lasting image that I would revisit time and time again. It's an impression that has since helped me to further understand our existence and purpose for being here. Today, we have advanced light years ahead of that first event. Now we have the ability to launch and land space shuttles to Mars and beyond. We push these transport units into space in order to accomplish various missions, from placing communication satellites into orbit around the earth to building space stations for human inhabitants and advancing our understanding of the universe through scientific experiments.

Now that space travel is familiar, and launching shuttles is no longer the miraculous event it was in 1964, such events have almost desensitized us to our miraculous existence within space. Religions have evolved over time to explain the concept of God as a creator, but I would like to exclude comparing which doctrine or theology is most accurate and whether science or mythology has played a role in our understanding of human existence. I am sure there are many scholars with books written to prove or disprove one philosophy over another. This book is my attempt to share my understanding. I have been on a spiritual journey my entire life. This has included taking part in various religions and studying the philosophy of many beliefs including Christianity, Judaism, Islamic, Muslim, Buddhist, Shintoist, Hinduism and other non-mainstream spiritual organizations that are attempting to teach people about our existence and the moral obligations that we have while living in this world. My belief is that all religions contain truth - however, there is only one truth that God abides by. God is God whether in the form of energy to some, a physical being to another, a spirit, a mountain, an ancestor, a prophet or however a religion may define the existence of God. In whatever form a civilization or religion may believe to be their God, we must respect all cultures and their associated beliefs about who they are and where they came from to now exist on this planet called earth. I have come to understand that God is a Supreme Soul that eminates energy throughout the universe and galaxies to infinity. This energy has no beginning and no end and has no measures with respect to time. God has existed for eternity as we have. The concepts of infinity and eternity may not be comprehendable by our finite minds which are limited to time. My discussion on this topic is outlined only to help you understand who your Creator is and not to delve into a discussion beyond this as that would require another book - perhaps several. One day, we will understand more, but there are many things that God has purposely kept from us so that our objective in life would not be distracted.

It was from this Soul Energy that God took part of himself and created a separate soul entity. This energy may be called intelligence, intention or spirit - whatever your terminology may be or belief may define it to be. The key point is that I don't want you to get caught up in semantics so much as to comprehend the common root essence of the fact that God created you from the very same energy that He himself is made of.

Dr. Wayne Dyer has identified Soul or Intention in his book, *"The Power of Intention"*. Dr. Dyer outlines that the characteristics of Beauty, Creativity, Kindness, Love,

Unlimited Abundance, Ever Expanding and Receptivity explain the nature of this intention energy described as God and the characteristics He portrays in all that He creates into existence. In other words, God has Intention to create within the realm of this energy that defines God and as we align ourselves with these seven faces of intention, we, in fact, align ourselves with the power of God. In the Holy Bible there are verses of scripture that talk about becoming one mind, might and strength with God. Because I grew up in the Christian culture, I will attempt to draw parallels to some of its teachings while I am sure that a Buddhist or Muslim could also find examples of this concept in the realm of their doctrine. Jesus taught people that He was here on earth to do the will of His Father. Jesus lived His life so as to create what his Father in Heaven would have Him create or do. Dr. Dyer has explained in his book that when we align our desires and become in tune with Intention or God, we can also co-create the world that we live in. I will explain this more in detail in the last chapter of the book, "Putting It All Together".

The main take-home message that I am trying to point out is for you to get a clear understanding of who you are. There are two ways in which we can look at our human experience. You can decide that you are either a Human Being having a limited Spiritual Experience, limited within a specific time frame of an eternal existence. Or you can see yourself as a Spiritual Being having a limited Human Experience. Considering your existence upon this earthly school is for a short 60-100 years in the timeline of eternity, the significance that we place on this existence in relation to eternity could define or distort our very purpose for existence. The reason that I am covering this in the first chapter of the book is so that you can clearly understanding where you came from and the relative significance of this pre-existence and post-existence based on your limited earthly experience. I also want to use this as a platform so that you may gain some insight into the issues of divorce and dysfunction that I experienced as a child. It is essential to start with a clear understanding of who you are and what you were exposed to as children. I will also help you understand how not receiving love and regard as a child may have affected your soul and it's capabilities to make decisions and choices throughout your life. Furthermore, I will describe what you can do to nurture this new soul as it grows from youth, into adulthood and eventual parenthood. I am taking you on a journey into the abyss where my life as a new soul born to earth became crushed. It fills me with dismay and sadness to know how a soul that is created by a God, the Supreme Power, can come into a world where separation, ill-treatment, and neglect can completely ruin the life of a child that is so innocent and helpless. It is my intention to describe to you what happens in divorce and how it destroys the essence of a soul's very purpose for being here on earth. I will also describe how to identify the dysfunctions that have developed from this experience so that you may correct the characteristics that have developed as a survival mode in the absence of love and regard.

Chapter 2: Childhood

Dear Children,

I was born April 15th, 1959 in Claresholm, Alberta, Canada to Ila Mae Jarvis and Robert Blair Hinckley. Grandparents of both sides of my family emigrated from the United States to homestead in Canada in the early 1900's. My parents had both previously married and divorced. There was one step-sister from my mom's previous marriage and two step-brothers from my father's previous marriage but both boys had died in infancy. Two older brothers also preceded me five and eight years earlier, respectively, making me the youngest of four children. What follows from here is an outline of the conditions that I grew up in and events that where significant to affect my soul and the feelings of trauma and distress that contributed to my future malfunctions. I will also outline some thoughts on what would have been a healthier solution to the situation that could have likely assisted in preventing many of the ill side effects that I developed as a result of these family conditions.

I don't recall a lot about my childhood but I do know that there were many more bad things that happened than good. My parents were married in 1951 at which time my step-sister was five years old. I came along eight years later and according to my sister there was much verbal and emotional mistreatment that occurred between my father and mother. My sister mentioned that when my parents fought verbally, she would take me and my brothers to another part of the house so we wouldn't be exposed to the noise and intense emotional exchanges, which I'm sure scared us as little children. I do remember on one occasion where I was sitting on my mother's knee and she was arguing with my father and my father was shouting at her while holding a butcher knife in his hand. I recall feeling that the anger was directed at me rather than at my mother who was behind me. It became a lasting image and sentiment that I carried well beyond that moment. When I was six years old I witnessed my mother's clothes packed and waiting on the front step at our farmhouse. She was to find them when she came home from the hair salon business which she had recently started. From this point on, I was traded back and forth between parents. At eight years of age my mother made the decision to marry someone she had met. She sent me back to the farm where my two brothers lived and sold her business and promptly moved away from me. She felt that I would be better off growing up in a relationship with my brothers than alone as an only child far away from them. The result of these decisions meant that I would barely have any contact with her for several years going forward. The other frightening reality was being dumped back on a farm where my emotionally and verbally abusive father was trying to run the operation while being a single parent to three children. Rather than go into details about the conditions of cruelty, I will expand on how this affected me. Many of these living conditions exist in homes of divorce, along with addictions and neglect. I believe all such circumstances are intertwined into developing ill-treatment that will affect the life of children exposed to these, particularly when they are quite young - between the ages of three to twelve. These are very vulnerable years for a child, a time when they are expected to be protected and nurtured with love and regard. But in cases of abandonment, rejection, addiction, neglect, verbal abuse, emotional abuse and physical abuse - children develop survival techniques in order to protect themselves against this hurt and pain. Survival techniques are not limited to the childhood and adolescent years of course – they are often amplified and shape the young adult and become detrimental to future relationships.

I came to understand about these shortcomings more than thirty years after I had initially developed them as a means to survive. When I look back on my life as a teenager, young adult and eventual adult at a time when I would marry and begin my own family, I recognized the dysfunctional way in which I conducted my life. I know that these faults are not exclusive to my experience, so it is my hope that through greater awareness many people will recognize the reactions that may be associated with the initial event and can make changes that lead to a better lifestyle or in the very least to get professional counseling to overcome these challenges.

At six years old, and a child back on the farm, I felt let down in many ways. First of all, when my mother moved out of the family home her first instinct was to take me with her. She was not initially able to remove me from the farm when she gathered her clothes and personal items. So she came back later and pulled me into a car while I was playing outside with my next oldest brother. This closest sibling also had feelings of being left behind and was hurt by the fact that he had been abandoned by our mother taking me but not him. I was glad to see my mother again, and to be with her, but I also felt sad that my brothers and father would be left behind and I would be unable to see them. I don't remember too many of the details but I do recall that in the next two years I had very little contact with my brothers or my father. That act of wrenching me away from both of my brothers and my father likely left scarring impressions on them as well.

When I was eight my mother remarried and I was sent back to the farm and once again felt abandoned and rejected by my mother. I had somehow become a foreigner to my father and siblings and was subject to all sorts of verbal and emotional abuse. And for the following eight years of living on the farm I learned to mistrust, lie, people-please, control and to live in a lot of fear because of the constant conflict that occurred. One of the other most significant things that grew out of this experience was my ego and the feeling that if I could just have a successful family, unlike my parents, I would be successful in my life. You will later see how my blemished childhood contributed to the demise of the marriages I would later enter into.

I was extremely hurt by my parents' separation. That special bond of the united family that we are all familiar with before we come to this earth was completely shattered. There was no peace, love or harmony in our family home that I remember, only fighting and quarreling. After my parents divorced I came to mistrust people, particularly if I believed they were going to withdraw from their association to me. This lack of trust is the essence of why such conflict is challenging for children of divorce. These children experienced two parents have opposing views and the end result was separation of the family. The aspect of parents having different ideas is not damaging, but it is the association of divorce and separation that is connected to it as pointed out by Judith Wallerstein. I used to be very fearful of conflict in my marriage because I felt there was an underlying agenda which would end up in a divorce and I would lose my wife and children. I carried this fear into other parts of my life as well and it is interesting to note that division would also occur in friendships and other associations such as jobs. I recall getting very nervous about having conflicting discussions with employers and left feeling that I would lose my job and that is exactly what occurred. We manifest what we think - and because this scenario was on my mind, and the fear of losing my job was at the forefront of thought, rather than thinking of being successful and happy, I created the job loss as a self-fulfilling prophecy. This disconnection with work played out much like the marital divorces that I went through. Even when friendships didn't work out, I tended to discard them like trash rather than just acknowledge that there are differences of opinion and accept those differences with respect. This type of bridge burning eventually left me feeling alone with no one to turn to. Children of divorce are often not well equipped in understanding how to deal with conflict and accept it as a normal part of life. These children tend to lack the skill to be accepting of differences and able to work through relationships without incurring any long term damage to their overall conditions.

As well as losing trust in my parents, I began to lose trust in God and everyone I associated with in life. You may have experienced something similar because of some level of mistrust that occurred. At first you may have given people your full trust almost to the extent of being naïve because you wanted to trust them so much. However, when an event occurs where you are let down or you feel like your friendship is being treated lightly, an uncertainty is introduced and the relationship suffers. Our lives depend on having a relationship with a Supreme Being who gives us what we need on a daily basis whether that is our jobs, homes, food, clothing, relationships or good health. Where is the quality of our lives if we stop believing in a God which provides for all these elements – and so much more? Without a relationship with the Supreme Spirit a person starts believing that everything in life counts on their individual actions – this can appear to be a good or bad thing. Certainly we have to be motivated to make an effort in life but what also tends to happen is that someone who has suffered from the effects of divorce often tries to control all of the outcomes in every other aspect of their life. A child of such a break-up will often feel stranded, abandoned with everything happening beyond their control.

I believe this is where trained counselors need to work with these children to help them come to a level of acceptance regarding the situation that is occurring. I never had such wise input as a child so I learned to live with a great deal of internal pain instead. I held a strong belief that when I would be in the position to marry and have a family of my own, I wasn't going to let this situation occur and do everything in my power to make certain that I was in charge. This meant people-pleasing or doing whatever it might take to make every situation better – particularly when it posed a threat to a unified home. The problem with people-pleasing is that when you do this, you lose respect for yourself because you are not being honest about the person you really are. You attempt to become the person that you think other people will love and adore. In the "Power of Intention", Dr.Dyer talks about Intention giving back to you what you are giving out to others. Therefore, if you are sending out energy that you do not respect the person you are, because you are busy trying to be someone that you are not, you will soon find yourself in the company of people who do not respect you. This is why it is so essential to understand who you really are and build your foundation on the fact that you are a child of God, an heir to an eternal kingdom that will be yours after you experience this life.

Further to people-pleasing, you also develop a habit of lying to not only avoid conflict but also to give people the answer that you believe they want. To be a child of divorce you learn how to become 'more perfect' because if you just try a little harder you will make that parent happier to the point where there will be less conflict and life will be enhanced because you controlled the outcome to make it healthier. You also learned to lie to your parent because you believed there would be severe consequences to telling the truth. Children who experience a family break up learn to survive the experience by avoiding conflict because this divergence leaves them with feelings of abandonment and rejection. Therefore, to avoid such discord children of divorce lie, mistrust and people-please.

The subject that I will cover now will be to discuss what type of environment we need to provide for early childhood, to avoid these types of character dysfunctions from developing. Take some time to consider a newborn baby. This little person is innocent, joyful, energetic, alert and loving when all its basic needs are met. I believe that what a child needs is to have parents continue providing for them everything that God afforded them before entering this mortal world. The basis for a healthy existence is love and regard. When these conditions are provided for a child, essential elements are offered for this young being to develop healthy self-esteem. When we came from God's presence we felt this love and regard as well as many other virtues. This Source provided everything for us in unlimited abundance. This Supreme Spirit showed us that creative powers could provide all that we needed and everything that was created had beauty which could offer ultimate joy to our lives. This loving Source was receptive to our needs and provided everything in an unselfish manner with infinite love and kindness. There were no boundaries to limit this Source – it was ever-expanding. It provided everything that we needed, and as our needs grew the boundaries for fulfilling these needs also expanded.

As we come to appreciate what our condition was in the pre-mortal existence, we can better provide for infants coming to the families that we intend to create. When these conditions abound, the virtues of life are present in the home and children can enjoy a safe, loving and stable environment. The child who has come to the mortal world can continue to feel the security that they previously experienced with the Spirit Source. They can thereby have the confidence that they are carrying on a continuum of spiritual growth throughout their physiological and psychological human development. Parents tend to be cognizant of their child's needs for food, shelter and clothing but there is an even greater need to provide for the spiritual development of the soul. A roadblock to such insight is that parents have already developed egos which define them on the basis of status, material wealth, appearance and all other body conscious parameters. This would include examples like what kind of car they drive or how big their house is or what type of profession they have and how does society view who they are. Once this ego has developed within the self, we are then living by such self-worth parameters which predict our happiness and fulfillment. This type of attitude is then passed on to the off-spring so they too begin to focus on the ego as defining who they are. Some of the greatest individuals in the world, and I will use Jesus Christ as the example because of my Christian background, were portrayed as being born from humble beginnings – such as in a stable - and grew into a life that did not produce or intend fame and fortune. For Jesus, His life was simple. He merely taught people to love the Source and to do His will while upon this earth and while they were experiencing their limited human existence. The point that I am trying to make is that our world has become so focused on body consciousness that we have slipped into amnesia of the need for the more focused effort on soul consciousness.

There are many religions and philosophies that are trying to address this issue to better understand our human existence and relationship to God. As a result of the fighting and wars which have occurred because of religion, and the heated debates over which doctrine is correct, people have grown weary and confused as to who and what to believe - let alone having knowledge of their existence and purpose for being here. It is essential to have a solid understanding of who we are and our association with God, the Source of all creations. This awareness is integral to our efforts in comprehending what a child needs when they are born into this worldly existence. If a child can feel love and regard to the same degree they experienced in their pre-existence, they will believe the power within themselves, by the Source Power that intended them into this life. Such awareness will allow a child to appreciate they were co-created by their parents and a loving God. They will come to understand their true nature and the power within them - much like when Jesus was merely twelve years old teaching the Jewish Rabis in the temple about life and the meaning therein.

Chapter 3: Teenage Adolescence

Dear Children,

Teenage adolescence was an extraordinarily challenging period of my life – as it is for most youths. I am referring to the age period between twelve and seventeen years. These awkward and tumultuous years are further amplified by the media and the bombardment of influencing images and messages that young people receive. This is a time when the pressure of other teenagers and peers is so great. It is interesting to note that childhood is marked as the first twelve years of our lives and yet, in less than half that time we mature through puberty, establish meaningful friendships and develop an understanding of the society that we live in. This is a time when friends play an exemplary role and can make or break the future of the teenager.

By the age of twelve I had been living back on the farm with my father and brothers for about four years. I accepted the absence of my mother but as previously mentioned, had developed my own survival techniques. As a child on the farm, I learned many things about hard work and basic living. As the youngest child I was expected to clean the house, do the laundry, prepare meals and many other household duties. I also had my share of work in the field, driving farm machinery - focusing on getting crop work done in the warmer months as well as feeding cattle throughout the winter. It seemed that there was no lack of work and having the opportunity to develop a strong work ethic is something I will always appreciate. I value this strong work ethic even more now as I live in an urban city and often have a desire to leave the bustling metropolitan setting in order to escape to the mountains or countryside for a retreat. I learned to play hockey in the winter and that was the extent of extra-curricular activity and entertainment. I spent a lot of time with my friends from school and it seemed that most occasions were consumed with drinking alcohol and smoking tobacco. It seemed to be the main form of amusement, and as the years went on the intensity of drinking and partying left me wondering if there was any thing else to do besides work and party. This was a time when my friends had a lot of influence on me, but I didn't have a father and mother working together to give me guidance on morals and values - including respecting my body and health. I was not inspired by my teachers and therefore did not perform well academically. Essentially, I didn't have parents that stressed the importance of education. Somehow my father just assumed that we would all continue the family farming business and there was really no other choice in the matter. I didn't have any exposure to outside interests or opportunities until I ran away from the farm at age 15. At that time my life was out of control. I didn't have a firm set of values or morals, let alone an understanding of the meaning of life. I'm not sure if my father really had a concept of why we exist either, but if he did, I could definitely have used some direction at this critical period of my life. But I was unable to ask such questions or reach for help and my father appeared so consumed with running the farm and raising three boys, there seemed to be no time to even discuss such a trivial topic. From the age of eight until I was 15, the main focus of my life was the loss and division that had occurred within our family. As this separation had never been resolved, I continuously held a desire to find my mother, feeling that if I could do this, things would be much better. However, even when I ran away from the farm to go and live with my mother, it was too late to correct the unhealthy lifestyle that I embraced. I entered into a high school in an urban setting but only stumbled through the first year, eventually dropping out. I had very low self esteem and found myself gravitating towards other kids that felt the same way about themselves. They were also children that had received no direction in life and found refuge in alcohol and drug abuse. These habit-forming substances continued to pull me downward along with other low energy activities that I was involved in. By age 17 I abandoned school to go into the working world. In hindsight, I believe it was a time when I should have been excelling academically, learning about the world and who I was and what I wanted out of life. But the lack of guidance and the absence of a unified home to reinforce such pursuits pushed me towards a very different path.

When I think about teenage years, I think about an imagination with endless possibilities. What a great period in one's life! There is no better time to experience life and several advantages allowing for this. First of all, you have grown through the childhood years when you were very dependent on your parents for all of your needs and direction. Safe shelter, food and clothing were provided with likely only a mere exchange of mild responsibility in the home. Cleaning your room, doing some household chores and helping out is a small tradeoff for what you are able to get in return. The teenage years are a time to explore and apply those elementary fundamentals of learning to everyday living.

When I considered the biggest factors for inhibiting my teenage development, I came to understand that influences in my life either helped or hindered my growth and happiness. It wasn't until some 30 years later that I would realize the factors that had deterred me from a healthy teenage development. A few years ago, I read a very influential book called "***Power vs. Force***" by Dr. David Hawkins. In this book, Dr. Hawkins has documented years of research correlated to human consciousness. Through kinesiological testing, he identifies that every type of sensory experienced in life can be categorized as something that either strengthens or weakens human existence. He goes further to say that the sensory that strengthens us as humans, called positive attractors, can and will attract other constructive sensory to promote a healthy consciousness. On the other hand, sensory that weakens human existence, named negative attractors, creates other negative sensory which ultimately engages damaging human consciousness. When I looked at his table titled, "Map of Consciousness", I came to realize that most of my teenage years were spent in low energy zones which produced negative attractors. These types of activities encouraged me to feel anger, hate, enslavement, withdrawal, anxiety, blame, guilt and shame. Dr. Hawkins identifies that smoking, drugs, alcohol, inappropriate television programs, and inappropriate sexuality can all be factors in weakening the human consciousness. Alternatively, any positive sensory that we experience in society like trust, optimism, acceptance, understanding, love, reverence, joy, serenity, peace, bliss, enlightenment, we can be assured that these types of sensory will produce a high energy experience and create positive attractors and thereby encourage other affirmative sensory. The take home message is that whatever we associate ourselves to in life, particularly during very vulnerable stages such as childhood and teenage years, can either weaken or strengthen us - which results in other similar experiences coming to us. A common analogy here would be parents telling their children that it is so important to have good friends that will influence their lives for good.

I know that as a teenager, life has many challenges. There is a great deal of physical and emotional development occurring. From physiological changes, to emotional transformations - all of these adjustments influence the development of character. Teenagers are exploring, trying to figure out who they are, what they feel, and who they want to be. This is a time when many influences play a factor. This is also a time when parents can offer authority and have an important role. I believe the relationship that a teenager has with their parents is directly correlated to the experience that they had as a child. Trust is developed in the parent-child relationship so when the child becomes a teenager, even when there may be a draw to self discovery over the parent direction, the parent's earlier influence will play a major role in helping the teenager choose between negative or positive energy. If the parent first emmites positive energy, the child will learn to seek such energy and of course, the opposite is also true. This is why the environment within the household is so critical when the new born child is developing and has such a profound impact through to the teenage period. Parents have a responsibility to their teenagers to expose them to positive activities such as sports, hobbies, associations and relationships that can have a constructive influence or effect. This is not a time to be bias and prejudice against other teenagers that did not have a positive energy experience in their homes. If the teenager gravitates towards another who has come from a dysfunctional environment, this is an opportunity to emit high energy into this teenagers life by bringing them into the realm of your positive family. This is an opportunity to charge this soul with encouraging influence. Such constructive input may be required frequently, such as a transfusion for a recovering patient, but in the end, much good will occur for both teenagers as they will equally benefit from the experience. As the teenager is able to have regular contact with these high energy experiences, they will come to see themselves in this light and will want to seek out other positive associations to add to their energy field. Deep inside themselves they will come to know what it is that they want in life because they have come to know who they really are.

I would strongly urge every teenager to be vigorous at discovering the many wonders of this world. With the advent of the internet, there is absolutely nothing that isn't available for learning. I highly urge you to seek after things of interest that promote a high energy experience. These types of experiences will give you joy and fulfillment in learning. They will provide opportunities for growth and development as you learn new skills. They will help you to understand leisure and activities that may be sports-based or offer you exercise and outdoor enjoyment to be in the world that God created for you. We are meant to explore this world, not just sit at home, looking through a window wondering if it was really meant for our benefit. Each day should be filled with marvel and amazement about our existence and the gift we have to interact with others on a daily basis. All things are creations and contain the same energy that you possess to make them alive and functional. All energy is designed to interact for our human experience.

Chapter 4: Young Adulthood

Dear Children,

I will start my description of young adulthood at age 17. I had been in the workforce for two years by now and was enjoying my life as I knew it, surrounded by thirty fellow co-workers in an electrical wholesale business. It is somewhat ironic but this company was like a family to me. I associated with fellow employees outside of the work hours and even attended company picnics and other special occasions throughout the year. While I might have gained a certain discipline for being responsible within my job, my lifestyle outside of work was a continual party, with drinking, smoking and using illegal drugs. I had many female associations but the relationships did not last long. Overall, I was a person with very little focus in life, living paycheck to paycheck and without any interests outside of the short blasts of immediate gratification. I used drinking as a crutch to aid my communication and social capabilities as I had learned throughout my teenage years and growing up on the farm. Bars, nightclubs and all-night drinking were the routine on weekday evenings and weekends. I had no idea at that time that there was a whole world out there to explore and learn what I wanted out of life. I was trapped in my low energy addictions. This lifestyle carried on for another four years and unfortunately the most I can tell you that I did with my life was progress within this small family organization to advance my career. This is the first time in my life I had to interact with people on an intelligent basis without drinking or taking some kind of drug to give me self confidence. I still remember the first customer's door that I drove up to when I was promoted to be an outside salesman. I was terrified at the prospect of having to go and talk to them so I just kept circling the block with my car. I never knew before this incident that I had such inhibitions and low self-esteem. I never knew what it was like to grow up in any other home so I had no idea that this type of self-confidence needed to be nurtured within the family and ideally developed throughout my growing years. For the first time of my life, I was starting to realize how little interest I had developed in anything in life. Eventually, I did go into the customer's office and I did complete the sale I had been entrusted to accomplish. This was my first step at breaking out of my shell to realize that I did have a voice and an opinion. I also realized that what I said could matter to someone and I grew to become a valued employee within the company. My confidence and spirits were lifted. This did not last long though, as a startling event changed the course of my life forever.

At age 21, my father passed away and I was devastated. My family, or what I considered my family, just disappeared. Even though my mother and step-father still lived close to me, I did not think of them as my primary family unit. Both of my older brothers were also shocked into the realization that the single care giver who raised us had suddenly left our lives. It was as if both parents had been killed in a car accident. There was also the responsibility of the family farm that would require managing and working. I left the adopted family that I had come to know through my job, to return to the farm, to assist my brothers in carrying on with the family business. Throughout this time of shock and confusion I had a continual feeling there was something significant that I was missing in my life – beyond the loss of my father - but I couldn't put my finger on it. The family that I never had was long since forgotten. I was empty inside and I started searching. This inner search would lead me to another type of family that characterized the next phase of my life.

When I look back and examine my young adult life, I see a continuation of the same kind of energy and activities that had been initiated in my teenage years. One of the values of developing good friendships as a youth is that it is the first chance to develop a community or relationships outside of our immediate family. Not only was the misdirection of my teenage years a contributing factor to my overall unhappiness, but the community that I had come to know from childhood was also lost. It required a great effort to start all over again, building new relationships in the city while living with my mother and step-father. Because my childhood and teenage experiences were so dysfunctional, I felt a great embarrassment in thinking about returning to the farm or the community that knew I had run away years prior. Obviously, this is another important factor for children to be considered when moving from one area to another. We tend to think about what is important to our careers as parents, often with very little consideration for the children and the dramatic changes they will have to be adapted to, should a major move be required. The positive friendships that are created in elementary, junior high and throughout our high school years are integral in a child's development and the basis of relationships that may be retained for future years – even a lifetime. Many of these associations become even more significant when attending post-secondary educational institutions. In the book "*Sacred Contracts*" written by Caroline Myss, I searched for some comfort and meaning to a recent loss of a very special relationship in my life. Her points support several facts around my belief in a pre-existent world, where we as spirit creations lived as brothers and sisters. She also identifies a beautiful portrayal of a pre-ordained mission that each of us take into this mortal world by making a sacred contract with those spiritual individuals whom we lived with previously and were also meant to play a significant role in our mortal experience. My first thought to this is that if we had a spiritual connection to specific individuals before being intended into this earthly existence, then how much more important is their association when we do make contact with them in life? It's a significant concept to remember.

As a child of divorce, one of the survival techniques my ego developed was to give someone a chance to be in my life, but if they let me down, they could not be trusted again. If they gave me any suspicion that they were going to hurt me in any way, they could not be kept as a friend. In many ways this is why most of the close friendships that I had throughout my teenage and young adult years never lasted. Because I had lost my ability to trust as a child, I did not possess this vitally important characteristic to develop healthy long-lasting relationships. I had also learned very well how to tell people what they wanted to hear and to gain their favor by being the type of person that was required by my peers and fellow workers. My ego had grown resilient throughout the years and had served well to protect me from being hurt. The biggest problem however was that it wasn't until later in life that I discovered that ego is an enemy to God. This literally meant that the bigger my ego became, the further I distanced myself from this divine creator and source energy.

Even as a young child, I always had an internal sense of the existence of a God or Supreme Being. I would find myself in circumstances as a child complaining to God when things did not turn out my way but also saying thank you to God when something good happened in my life. I realized that rather than have faith with the situations that occurred, life as a child of divorce had expanded my ego into believing I could control the outcome of all circumstances. It was later that I would understand that while in a recovery mode, I would be required to 'Let go and let God', a popular phrase used by many recovering addicts so that the power and influence of a Source Energy greater than themselves may be allowed to work within their lives. This is partially the path that I followed after my father passed away. My direction led me to organized religion which provided two things that were missing in my life. First and foremost, the family that I always wanted but never had, once again appeared in the form of organized religion which contained brothers and sisters that treated each other with love and respect. But more important, it was the vehicle that would lead me to formal training about spirituality and the need we have in our lives to trust God. Little did I know at that time that learning to trust God meant learning to trust myself.

Chapter 5: Adulthood

Dear Children,

Let us begin this portion of life at age 21. Even though we generally define adulthood at age 18, everyone matures at different rates based on the experiences they have had up until that time, therefore, every individual I believe becomes an adult in their own time. For this reason, age difference in people becomes less significant based on the maturity that people have acquired through knowledge, experiences and the childhood nurturing they received within their families of origin. For me, because my family environments offered little nurturing and the experiences that I had were very low energy and didn't allow me enough diversity in my knowledge, I was lacking a great deal of maturity. Through high energy experiences we have in life, we are able to develop self-confidence and capabilities that propel us to endeavors that require greater effort. At age 21, I had very little experience to attribute to my personal portfolio, but that would soon change with the church organization that I embraced.

When I became a Christian, I began to realize that there are many people outside of a biological family unit that can demonstrate love and respect. I felt an instant acceptance into the church as I began to further understand the principles of Christianity. I learned that the way to be happy was to live a life emulated by Jesus - understanding His life was an important part of the process to gain peace in my own life. This type of association and scholarship is accredited to high energy. I had been deprived for this knowledge and became a sponge soaking up the gallons of liquid sushine to fill my soul that was empty and inadvertently filled with darkness related to the low energy activities that I had participated in for most of my life up until that point. As Dr. Wayne Dyer indicates in his book, *"The Power of Intention"*, knowledge from the Source of Intention is light, which he also correlates to Dr. David Hawkins' findings of high energy or positive attractors. In contrast to this, darkness or lightless environments occur in a life that is based on low energy sensory association, or what Dr. Hawkins calls negative attractors. The teachings from the Bible, Tao Te Ching, Tora, Talmud, Kabala and Koran are all writings that produce high energy to varying degrees. All of these great works offer enrichment for the soul but it is the criticisms of man, and the debates of which doctrine is correct, that remove the positive experience someone might have through a deep understanding of these theologies. It is interesting to note that where light exists, one cannot create darkness without closing their eyes, but where darkness exists one only needs light to eliminate the darkness. When we become associated with light and knowledge it teaches us to embrace happiness. The joy provided by our Creator cannot alter unless we close our eyes to the enlightenment and deny the truth that we have come to know. The action of walking away from that light is to shut our eyes and accept darkness and the low energy sensory that weakens us. Because it is a negative attractor, it will draw more low energy or darkness to our lives. This is why it is so critical to influence a child with as much high energy as possible within the family of origin. If that has not occurred however, it is not too late. It is never too late to decide to recognize God, who is the Source Power to deliver us.

After a year and a half of continual exposure to the uplifting energy associated with Christianity, I still held a desire to experience what the Spirit Source wanted for me and to make up for lost time. I made an application to volunteer as a missionary to teach Christianity and assist people in attaining more light and knowledge within their own lives. I did this for eighteen months and was soon to realize the joy one receives in selfless service and the unexpected blessings of greater light and knowledge that would come back to me as a result of helping others. As a high school dropout, with very little education and experience, I would soon learn the power that existed to give me the ability to learn the Japanese language and build up faith and courage to leave the North American continent and live in an Asian culture so contrary to what I had grown up in. I had many struggles and challenges, but overlooking my own weaknesses, I came to understand that we live in a world created by a loving God. I also came to understand that as we have faith in ourselves and the purpose of our lives, the powerful Source will help us acquire awareness beyond what even the human mind can comprehend.

After returning home from living in Japan, I finished my high school learning through adult training courses to allow me to enter post-secondary education. I first studied mechanical engineering and then went on to study biochemistry, then further learned about the principles of teaching in the education department. My complete emersion into selfless service and a life transfusion of high energy while living and serving in Japan had matured me to the point of acquiring the self-confidence and capability to gain further light and knowledge. The illumination inside my soul was growing stronger and brighter each day, week, month and year as time went by. I was finally receiving the joy and fulfillment that I had never known before. I was now preparing for the next learning experience of my life.

Without completely understanding why I was becoming so much healthier from a spiritual standpoint at that time in my life, I began to realize the wonder of the world and universe. I remember standing outside of my home in Miyako Island, Japan, looking up to the stars at night recognizing that I was literally on the other side of the planet from my home in North America. I would have never have imagined that this is where my life would have led me in my childhood days. We can never know completely the path that our lives will take. I never planned on living in Japan as a missionary but I started to wonder again about life and whether we really do predict how our lives might be or was there a storyline or drama that we are meant to follow. I began to understand more clearly that we are directed by a loving Source who intended us, along with our parents, into this worldly existence. Was my purpose merely as an actor in this drama called life? Was I playing a role and able to interact with other souls for the purpose of growth and spiritual development on their part and mine? The thinking required at this point appeared to be too deep for me but the thought had flashed across my mind. I would not delve into a greater appreciation until a much later time when discovering the importance of the drama and how I would perceive my part and the role that I played.

I was starting to see the value of embracing good things in my life, and understanding that I had the capability to accomplish whatever I set out to do. I was now fully immersed in a spiritual family and completed my sacred assignment of volunteer work and post-secondary education - so what was next? I was informed after my mission the my next challenge in life was to get out there, find myself a companion, get married and have a family. Sounds pretty fundamental and stereotypical of life as we have generally come to know it, but this is where my complete lack of healthy experiences would hinder me greatly. My early life experiences of coming from a broken home and a family unit that had been torn apart did not lend to having a great deal of helpful insight when thinking about creating my own family. This is where I became very naïve about how to approach the institution of marriage and long-lasting love. One must be very cautious that everyone's understanding of life is not on the same level. I realize now that while the church had good intentions for my life and its future, and while I might be eager and willing to continue on a progression and enter into such a sacred obligation, I was lacking the understanding of courtship, loving companionship and how to evaluate a relationship. I did not have the maturity and mental faculties to appreciate what could be viable and what may be required to support each other emotionally, spiritually and intellectually. I was like a kid in a candy shop just gazing around at all the colors and potential flavors for a relationship and as soon as I saw the one that I thought looked good, I grabbed it. Before I knew it, I was married and in a serious commitment. And sure enough, that relationship ended in divorce – and I was repeating my greatest fear, perpetuating the plague of broken homes and family units in ruin. But not only would I take part in one ended marriage, I repeated this act again and in less than 10 years had two failed marriages and four displaced children in my wake.

After several attempts at marriage, I began to look more internally as to the root of the problem. Why were my marriages failing? I was trying to be a good husband, father and church goer but on the inside, I was feeling a great deal of pain and unhappiness. What was really going on? It would be 20 years later before my epiphany occurred and I would come to understand that being a child of divorce had set up a foundation to beget more of the same, and so the plague would continue. I began to realize that there was no coincidence on why the divorce rate was approximately 50% in North America and many so called modern societies. In fact, many experts believe the rate is sure to rise in the future.

After creating four beautiful children, my heart was broken knowing that they would suffer the effects of this plague within their own lives unless I could understand what was wrong with me and why I could not remain married. I was distraught in the knowledge that after only three to five years, each marriage would end, leaving children attempting to survive in single parent homes or homes with step-parents and boyfriends that had little or no affection for my children. There would only be separation, fighting and replicating what I had been through in my early years.

After much searching and contemplation for answers I entered into a recovery mode with the help of a psychological counselor who assisted me in rediscovering what I had lost as a child and how I would come to revive myself with new light and knowledge from the Source. This would not only enlighten me but also motivate me to write this book for your benefit, to understand the effects of divorce and how we can overcome the many challenges that it poses in our married lives in this 21st century. If we do not begin to understand and practice these principals, there will continue to be an escalating rate of divorce and associated dysfunctional problems reoccurring in the lives of our children. An often-quoted passage of the Bible outlines this understanding with "the sins of the fathers will be passed down to the children". This plague must be stopped and can only be halted with understanding through a comprehensive knowledge of its effects.

Let me elaborate more completely on a philosophy derived from the Hindu religion that I have come to understand

and apply in my life. Within the realm of this belief there is an awareness that five vices develop when we do not receive love and regard. These vices are anger, greed, lust, ego and attachment. They are the characteristics of "Maya"- otherwise known as "Illusion" in life. In comparison, as Christians we would call Maya the devil or adversary and there are surely many other names for this entity in other religions. I believe these five characteristics become engrained within a child of divorce, particularly in situations where the child has been neglected, abandoned, rejected, abused or any other traumatic event that has occurred where negative attractors have existed. Let's look at each one of these characteristics in the relationship of marriage and as a child of divorce. Let's remember back to Ms. Judith Wallerstein's finding that children of divorce are very sensitive to conflict and frightened at what the outcome of disharmony may result in. Every marriage has some type of conflict within it. That first year of marriage, commonly called the honeymoon phase, is often masked by the euphoric eros chemicals that are engaged after first meeting the love of your life. But differences of opinions soon emerge and depending on how well you evaluated the potential matches available to you, there may be more complications at resolving conflict with some of these companions than with other potential mates. When anger ensues, low energy prevails within the relationship and can serve to darken the light that was once ignited. Lust is another damaging characteristic of Maya, because it teaches to take, rather than to give. Lust is about satisfying one's own needs in contrast to fulfilling the needs of someone else. Therefore, if one spouse is more concerned about taking in the relationship rather than giving, the resultant feelings will leave the other spouse with a feeling of not being loved, once again reinforcing the very concept of why lust had originally developed within the soul of the child of divorce. Greed is all about wanting more and never being satisfied with what we have. I will talk about Soul Consciousness vs. Body Consciousness in more detail later but let me explain that greed has become all-consuming in our 21st century lifestyle because of the wealth and the affluence we have chosen. Our egos have developed through unhealthy environments and many of us have come to define who we are by our appearance, wealth, homes, cars and our status which has left us wanting even more. This continual desire for more, along with never feeling satisfied, creates conflict within the home and stress on the relationship. Attachment is an important concept when it comes to a healthy relationship. If the spouse has developed a need for attachment through an unhealthy childhood environment, this continues through to marriage which prevents either partner from growth on an individual level. Modern day psychology has defined this as codependency, and my feeling is reflective of Stephen R. Covey, a great American author. This well-know author outlines that we must first experience dependency as a child, then move on to independency as an adult and then progress to a healthy point of inter-dependency within a relationship. So here is how it plays out when it comes to attachment - if a child growing up in a broken dysfunctional home, let alone any malfunctioning home, is never allowed to experience independency because of the controlling nature of their shattered home life, the child will not develop a healthy ability to become dependent upon themselves. The low energy of these early years transfers through to adult years and into other relationships and marriages. People that walk down the matrimonial aisle or get into serious relationships without ever having had a chance to develop independency will likely become dependent on the significant person in their life, thus putting stress on the relationship. This will result in a power struggle between the two individuals and eventually require one of the parties to be submissive while the other dominates the relationship. Some people may believe that they prefer to be dependent on someone, but they will eventually become tired of the respect that is lost within the relationship. A healthy respect for oneself can only develop through an individual having had an opportunity to grow without any attachments. No strings attached as they say. Two individuals that have developed a healthy independence can then go on to develop a healthy inter-dependent relationship. Only on this basis can two people build a workable, non-attached contract that will not produce over-riding conflict in marriage.

So why is conflict so frightening for an adult that is a child of divorce? Ms. Wallerstein outlines in the "*Unexpected Legacy of Divorce*" that children who grow up in homes where there is a great deal of conflict, fair much better within the realm of their own marriages than children whose parents divorced. Children who come from broken homes believe this: when conflict occurs in marriage, unless it is understood, fully validated and supported that the relationship will stay in tack regardless of the differing opinions, the child will feel that these quarrels will end in divorce as well. These insecurities force the child to reconnect with early survival techniques which work in opposition to resolving the conflict. The first emotional response to conflict is a fear of abandonment and rejection. In my marriage, there was a continual verbal threat that my wife was going to divorce me, so I didn't have to even imagine this event happening because the words had been spoken and my greatest fear was perpetually being repeated in my ears.

Let's go through the fear cycle again for the child of divorce. So the first thing that happens is that the young person feels abandoned. In order to feel any control in their life they must now act to survive. They may start by lying and negating what they really feel just to please the dominating parent. They become people-pleasers doing all kinds of acts of martyrdom to prevent any type of rejection or abandonment and to try to control all outcomes. They also lose trust in the dominant parent even though it may appear that they are fine on the surface. These characteristics produce a lack in self-respect and this becomes predominant. And a person who has a lack of self respect cannot gain any admiration from other people let alone the spouse that they are trying to gain admiration from. We are created from the Source and this Entity will only give back to us what we are emanating. Therefore, a lack of self-respect will drive a person down into the low energy of human consciousness and will activate negative attractors. Not only is the infidel spouse now looking for love and regard which they did not receive as a child; they are also looking for fulfillment in the dwindling energy zones. Attempts to fill the void are made. This may include pornography, drinking excessively, drug abuse, eliciting for sexual relations outside of marriage and a whole host of other illusionary activities that are negative attractors. The most worrisome problem is that the adult that grew up as a child of divorce may not even understand why they feel empty and have such desires to fill the abyss. They possibly do not understand that deep within their hearts they likely do love their spouse but their marriage is now a downward spiral filled with lies and deception to the eventual destruction of what was once a beautiful creation. Furthermore, innocent children that were once intended into a wonderful home are now left to deal with the remains of a broken habitat and the cycle and sins of the parents will continue to another generation.

The significance of the attitude of this child of divorce is how the learned characteristics from childhood carry over to several areas of adult life. A relationship is a connection and there are many different types of associations including friendships and working relationships. Translating childhood sentiments to other relationships - for example in work, actions of lies and deception may also surface within the workplace. Failed friendships and job losses create a feeling of insecurity and compound even further to dishonesty. Adult children of divorce will continually try to control the outcomes in the workplace and friendships. These individuals often appear as very opinionated and unwilling to compromise for the well-being of the company or relationship as a whole. There may also be some manifestations of perfectionism or a need to control parts of their life and the lives of others. One of the most disheartening effects however comes in the need to control the outcomes of life. This translates into mistrust for life itself and for the Source which intended us here in the first place. One of the reasons for our existence is to gain faith in our Creator, a belief in our purpose and a willingness to accept all the drama which unfolds throughout our lives. We can only make the best decisions on a day to day basis. But there is great panic and anxiety in the adult which grew up in a broken home where they had little or no control over the outcomes of their unhappiness, the basis of their malfunctioning home. Being an adult and having to take on much more responsibility in your life can be very challenging unless you come to fully understand yourself and why you do the things you do. Even with such understanding, a marriage comprised of one or both individuals who grew up in a destroyed home will require a great deal of understanding, patience, love and compassion in order to create a successful matrimony and to bring healthy children into this world.

Chapter 6: Parenthood

Dear Children,

When I consider parenthood, I think of my life right now. With my children maturing into adulthood, I feel an overwhelming responsibility at this time of my life. As God has empowered me to write this book, He is also directing me to examine my life and understand if I was doing everything possible for the benefit of my children. Had everything that I wanted unfolded as I had planned or did I have to make adaptations for current situations in life? Was I being the best possible father and did I truly understand what my role and example would do for my children to develop into healthy adults? These were some of the questions I began to ask myself in a search for deeper meaning in life related to parenting. I thought my situation seemed rather unusual being that my children resulted from two different marriages. And by this time in my life I had attempted to focus on my career development and personal needs. I had moved to California and pursued employment in the bio-medical industry. I loved many aspects of my life

– not to mention the consistency of beautiful weather and surroundings – but something inside me continued to gnaw at my consciousness. I wondered how would I, as a parent, ever possibly be successful at having some sort of influence in my children's lives, let alone have any type of contact with them? And when I finally did look at leaving my career in California to relocate to Canada, and do whatever I could for employment, I discovered that all of my children had moved back to the same city, not to mention within five miles of each other. I knew that moving back would not be an easy task, mainly the effort of starting all over again, but also that this was what I was supposed to do. I felt a deep conviction within my heart that regardless of the circumstances, an essential purpose in life was to be a good father. This has all sorts of challenges when the father is not living in the home of the children, but I knew that my motivation to have this contact was for a much deeper meaning than what seemed obvious. God was directing me in this path and I was answering the call. I knew that if our Supreme Source's main concern was for us to be in sync with the lives of His spirit children, then as a father also, my main concern should be focused around my children's lives and helping them understand who they are and their purpose for being here.

It is essential that I outline what kind of parents I had and the type of example that was set for me. This was a very hard section to write because of the traumatic feelings that I had growing up, however, I have attempted to convey that even after all the heartache and sorrow that I went through, I still have a deep love and respect for my parents for intending me into this life, to have an opportunity to experience mortality. At one time in my life I felt angry and embittered by their actions and irresponsibility, however, as I became aware of my own life, I began to feel acceptance and a need to forgive so that my own life could be healed. Each individual, in whatever family of origin they come from, goes through an evolutionary development. I am not in any position to judge what they might have gone through in their own lives, nor do I know how this affected them and their capabilities to act as parents and responsible individuals. So when I portray the parents that I had, I only want to make an association of the findings that I have discovered and correlate them to the solutions that I believe will assist you to become better parents than they had been to me. In turn, I hope to convey how I could also have been a better parent, and ultimately that you will be a much better parent than I or my parents have been.

From the very early embryotic development of my life, I did not receive a celebratory welcome. In speaking with my sister on one occasion, I was curious to know what kind of familial existence prevailed when I came into our home. I already mentioned the violent, fighting atmosphere that dominated our home even before I came along. My parents had been married for about nine years - enough time to have my two older brothers before my birth. I have no doubt that there must have been some type of happiness between my parents at one point of their lives. I remember my mother telling me that she met my father at a dance hall where they spent many hours together enjoying this social activity. They married and my father took her and my step-sister to the farm where our family ancestors had settled roughly forty years earlier from the Midwestern United States. I don't have much detail on their relationship but I know they had friends that they liked to go to events with. I recall seeing many photographs of them with their friends having fun. Suffice to say that there must have been a reasonably good beginning to the relationship. They went on to pro-create three more children but by the time I came along, things were not so harmonious any more. The loving home that once began turned into a domicile of anger, ego and attachment that produced domestic violence and terror. Not only did their bad examples hurt me and my siblings, but they caused us great fear and confusion about our security and well being. My parents split up when I was six, leaving me with a feeling of insecurity and not trusting life. My mother remarried within two years of my parent's separation, which left their relationship even more contentious than before. After the divorce I don't recall them ever conversing or being amicable to each other. In fact, from the time that I was taken from our farm at age six, I don't believe my parents ever spoke to each other again. They seemed to just carry on with their lives never realizing the fact that their children were a byproduct of their once loving relationship. It seemed that just because they decided to end the association, it left question in my mind regarding who I really was. The loving parents that once intended me into this life were no longer together and I would somehow have to redefine myself in this world, and figure out what my purpose would be with little or no direction from any parent. My father provided food, shelter and clothing for us, but other than that, we pretty much had to fend for ourselves. I don't remember my father teaching me anything about life and what my understanding should be. All that my brothers and I appeared to be were work-hands on the farm. We did what we were told in order to get the work accomplished. Doing farm work was the first priority, then came schoolwork and any other activities. One of the few things I recall as being enjoyable was when we went to the city to visit my grandmother and uncle. We were able to play with the neighbor children and spend many hours in leisure - unlike our many commitments and constant work at the farm. It seemed like the farm was all about work and never about time as a family, learning and growing together or having fun together. There was very little joy in being in our family. It seemed that so much time was spent laboring, that even my brothers and I never really got to know each other. We did not learn how to play together and we have no fond memories of vacations together. My Uncle Bill, whom I will always love, spent time with us when we came to the city. He did not have any children and perhaps looked at us as part of his own family. I have a great fondness for this uncle and I am sure my brothers would echo this same sentiment.

So what is parenthood and what responsibilities are associated to it? Well, first of all let's look at the ultimate parent, being God as our Father in Heaven. There is no coincidence that our world was created in the manner in which all creations are formulated into this life. We know that for this life to exist, pro-creation is an absolute necessity. The family is at the center core of all living mammal creations. We start with a man and a woman, for if you desire to pro-create; this is the unity that must occur. In religion we have come to recognize the Divine Source as being only a Father of all spiritual creations. In other spiritual doctrine, God is both our Father and Mother but at this point of not being fully enlightened, suffice to say that we experience Heavenly Parenthood in one form or another from which all of life has been modeled after. Consider for a moment what life with God as our Father and Mother might be like and how this may assist in our understanding towards a correct parenting philosophy. When men and women fall in love and begin the course of their lives together, they become one in unity and effort with regards to how they will move forward as a family unit. Some couples decide to have no children or are not able to have children. Other couples decide to have one or two children and others have many. Whatever your decision to have children may be, you must be comfortable with what you and your companion decide. There are numerous elements to consider regarding creating children but beyond the thought of whether one will be able to financially provide for these offspring, is the commitment that whatever proceeds forth from this decision is irreversible. The thought of children begins deep within our subconscious minds. We have been influenced by many factors throughout our lives and even from our premortal experience we have developed a checklist of pros and cons to having our own families.

When we were created by Godly Parentage we knew that it was good. From the Bible we know that all the things that God creates are good, so I believe that before the world even existed or began as we know it, we were created as spiritual children of a Divine Source. Since we were formed, all of us, in this premortal existence, lived in a family before we ever came to this mortal experience we call life. We had unlimited joy in our spiritual lives as brothers and sisters to Godly parents. I expect that in our Heavenly existence we were nurtured much like we are required to provide for our children in this life. Food, shelter and clothing may not be needed in a spiritual energy form, but let's consider what The Source might have provided for our understanding and benefit. We see that in life, we progress through an evolutionary understanding based on experiences and the things that we have learned associated to this. I remember as a small child touching a hot element on the stove top and feeling great pain, fortunately without long term scars or disabilities. This was an experience that helped me to understand the dangers of close contact with open heat sources. I also remember learning how to skate as a child. First falling to the ice almost incessantly, then using a chair to push along the slippery surface and finally accomplishing the act of balance, to allow me the freedom of movement, on the sheet of frozen ice. If our mortal existence reflects our premortal existence only in an imperfect form, then I believe we had experiences and were taught by Divine parents who loved us and knew that we would require pre-mortal knowledge to guide us in a mortal existence. I will not speculate any further on what that knowledge may have been but believe we must have passed the examination requirements to allow us passage to this mortal university of life.

We look at life and notice that generally in a natural state, most things are being created. Without effort the seedling falls on the fertile ground to arise into another plant. Living animals in the world are not as concerned about doing an economic evaluation of whether they can provide a huge house and nice cars and motor boats for their offspring to enjoy, so much as their natural instinct is propelling them to multiply and replenish the earth. It seems that in the case of human families, we have tried to reverse this natural process of creation and propelled an unnatural force of destruction within the confines of this sacred human unit. Can you imagine God or our Divine Parentage creating us as spiritual children and then deciding that they had made a mistake and would reverse the original creation. This just does not exist in a natural state in life so why would this exist in our premortal existence. The tree does not root, sprout and grow above the surface of the soil and then revert back to being a seed when the cold winds blow with snow covering the branches and then it decides this world is not the right place, and then revert back to roots and then a seedling. There is one direction for the process of creation. Whatever our Supreme Source created was what was intended and there was no mistake made in the very beginning.

So let's carry this thought through to the process of parenting. If we had all grown up in a perfect family, much like the one that God provided, and remembered the way in which we were taught and nurtured in a heavenly existence, chances are we would do a much better job at parenting because of the perfect model that would have been provided for us. The problem is that we live in a world where relationships, marriages and families are being torn apart and literally destroyed. This is the model that is being imprinted on our minds so how can we expect to know how to proceed within our own families. When talking with many young people about marriage and having children, there is a feeling of skepticism and disbelief in the possibilities of creating a successful family. However, this has not altered out innate desires which we originally formed while in the preexistent state. Deep within us all, is a desire to be happy and have peace in our lives. This state is experienced as we existed before our mortal birth. We experience happiness through the union of marriage and complete commitment to allow that environment to create children to fulfill our lives, to teach, nurture and love in a world created with beauty for our benefit.

So let's look at a marriage that has been defined as a healthy beginning and the couples as they are now looking at how to provide an environment for the baby that has had its beginning as an embryo. There are so many parenting books available to know how to be a good parent. Well, the fact is that you are already a great parent if you understand that you came from the best spiritual parenting in the universe. The key is to focus on the spiritual form rather than the temporal form. The developing embryo is receptive to all sensory available at the time of development according to most embryo development studies. The spiritual soul of that embryo is completely receptive to all energies available to it. So now we get back to the studies by Dr. David Hawkins in *"Power vs. Force"*. For the most part, if we have grown up in a healthy environment, either we had parents who regulated the exposure to positive or negative attractors or we have been taught to understand what kind of influences are presented when associating with high or low energy. This is still the same in application when it comes to parenting. The environment that we expose to the fetus will affect the way in which it develops from a spiritual standpoint. Thus, as a parent, if I expose my children at any stage of develop to low energy which produces negative attractors, they will imbibe this energy within the realm of their human conscious development. Alternately when exposing children to high energy which will produce positive attractors, they will benefit by this mere association and also emit positive attractors to external stimuli as well. I would highly recommend reading this amazing book which was one of the key information sources that helped me to realize the effect of divorce that occurred to me in my own life and how this effect carried through to my own married life and role as a parent.

Because these forces of low energy had been such an influencing factor in my life, dysfunctional characteristics were formed that I reverted to when conflict arose within my marriage. If you can understand this concept, you can understand why you may be reacting or responding in the way you do. I believe that the degree in which characteristics develop are in direct correlation to the degree of exposure to either high or low energy while growing from childhood to adulthood. Generally speaking, we have to be healthy ourselves to be good parents. We cannot blame our past and attempt to take reprieve regarding our job as parents. We must take responsibility for our understanding and healing now. And we must also be conscious of our children's development to save them from this plague that has existed since the beginning of humankind. When we begin to understand the roots of the problem, like weeds in a garden, we can begin by differentiating between the good plants and the less desirable ones. For it is the good plants with elevating energy that we want to keep and thereby have the ability to enjoy an abundant harvest. As we begin to understand the weeds that are choking out the nutrients to the garden of our souls, we can selectively remove the low energy attractors that propagate contention and conflict within the institution of marriage. The key is to understand that weeds grow out of divorce. After half a century of living, I have come to understand those weeds and the destructive force they bring. I have been able to process this information in order to grow a new kind of garden.

Divorce has always existed, there is no question of that. But the rates by which couples who have come together under the covenant of a marriage and then decided to separate is a contemporary problem, plagues our society. Divorce rates have grown from 10% since the 1960's, to an astounding 50% only 50 years later. It is difficult to extrapolate this rate over the next 50 years but we can certainly understand a trend that is ultimately out of control and that is destroying so many of God's creations that were originally intended for a joy-filled life. It is my intention, to share this understanding that you may learn from my experience so you may benefit and gain complete joy, peace and contentment.

As you read these things and become aware of the dysfunctions that occurred in your life as a result of being a child of divorce, it is my hope that first, you will acknowledge the human dysfunction that exists within. I hope that this knowledge will be respected by not only you but also the companion that you have chosen in your life. Through mutual understanding you can nurture a feeling of love and security for all immediate family members, and a strategy can be developed to assist those affected to develop alternative reactive modes. Knowledge is power. So it is with this knowledge that you have the power to transform your life. It is with this power that you have the ability to be a good parent and to provide your children with a much healthier environment to have their beginnings grow from, so that they will also experience love and joy. This knowledge is for you and your spouse to apply to your marriage, so that there will be power to respect the environment from which you were originally developed and possibly for them as well, if they also grew up in a divorced home. The root understanding is that children of divorce cannot deal in a healthy manner with conflict. If you can grasp this, it will help you realize that great love and understanding will be required to preserve the creation of the wonderful beginning that God created. A pronounced passage from the Holy Bible to remember is, "What God bringeth together, let no man put asunder." I believe in marriage. I believe the Source intended us to devote ourselves to each other and to stay committed and respect the covenant that we willingly entered into. I believe if we know how to develop healthy relationships and identify potential for a long lasting communion, that these marriages will have the potential to last forever. The children which are created from these unions will then have a never-ending blessing that will last throughout this world and the eternal life to come.

Part 2:
The Age of
Enlightenment

Chapter 7: Who Am I?

Dear Children,

Now that we have gone through the various stages of human development and looked at how my life as a child of divorce was in comparison to the many spiritual teachings that I have acquired, let's now focus more specifically on the age of enlightenment. At some specific age in our human development, each person comes to a clearer understanding of life. Each can take a different path, some of which can offer great joy and others present great pain. As they say, "Life is filled with ups and downs", and let me use an analogy that came to me of this very purpose.

I had been serving as a volunteer missionary in Japan for a period of 1.5 years. One of the areas that I was assigned to was the city of Naha on a southern island of Japan called Okinawa. On this island was an American military installation and I had the opportunity to meet many wonderful people who were living and working overseas to serve their country. I met one family and spent the Christmas holidays with them and was introduced to a friend of the family by the name of Bill. While visiting the military base, Bill showed me around the various training areas in the facility, which was primarily used to prepare pilots that flew F-18's. I have a vivid recollection of an event that would change my understanding of life and develop a greater appreciation for this character-building process. Bill asked me if I had ever flown an F-18 and I naturally laughed at the suggestion - I think he already knew the answer to that question. He then asked me if I would like to try flying an F-18. My eyes flew wide open and I answered with an emphatic, "Yes!" Bill was a co-pilot and flew one of the F-18's at the military installation on a regular basis, so I figured that he must have some pretty good connections to accomplish this. Well, it wasn't quite as I expected but still a very exciting experience. What unfolded next is that I entered one of the training simulators – designed completely to replicate the cockpit of an F-18. After Bill closed the cover, I didn't have any other thought. My mind filled with the present moment – and the fact that I was actually going to fly this amazing jet. Bill went over an explanation of the controls and what was required to have a successful flight. He communicated to me with a headset outside of the simulator and also had the ability to create any type of weather patterns to affect the flight of the aircraft. So with my one hand on the control stick and the other on the slide control for thrust, I taxied the aircraft out onto the runway. Bill instructed me to align the plane with the runway marker and push the thrust control forward. I could feel movement in the cockpit to simulate the acceleration of the aircraft and saw the air speed indicator increasing. After I had reached a certain airspeed Bill then instructed me to pull back slowly on the control stick to lift the nose of the plane up to the horizon. He indicated that if this angle of increase was attempted too steep, the aircraft would stall, then crash and burn, so the first aspect to takeoff was to have an acceptable rate of increase for a safe flight. As the aircraft was climbing, I could see the altimeter displaying the increased altitude. Once I reached about six thousand feet, Bill explained that in combat one of the strategies used to accelerate the speed of the plane was to direct the nose downward towards the earth. I did this on his command and soon experienced the significance of the law of gravity – the aircraft surged forward as accelerated velocity took over. After dropping to about three thousand feet, I then pulled back on the control stick as instructed by Bill, which seemed to slingshot me at twice the acceleration that I had originally experienced in the initial take-off. When we had found an elevation where I could level the plane, Bill created all types of weather situations including lightening storms so I could see the effect on the plane functions as well as the indicators. It was a truly unbelievable experience. And little did I know that flying an F-18 would help me to understand life when God would show me that the same principles are used in this earthly event.

Consider life, similar to a sine wave that curves up and down at regular intervals along a certain pathway. Now take the end of the sine wave and stretch it far above the level at which it originally started. This would almost look like a staircase that ascends however, the steps would also include dips that create valley-like descents. Similar to the F-18 and the function of increasing acceleration, God accelerates our growth and learning in this life by using a similar principle. Within the span of 60-80 years we are required to live the life that was intended for us. Some souls are in this school of life longer and some are here for a shorter period of time, but be assured, you will remain in this life for as long as God intends you to experience the drama as it unfolds. We sometimes mourn the loss of loved ones at an early age when we feel their life has just begun. This is because our minds can only comprehend the current existence and without any knowledge of the life before or after, we fear that this life is the only life there is to live. Let me assure you, I am certain that if we will place our trust and faith in a Divine Source who created this world and intended us to come here to live - in a God who was willing to pay our tuition for the University of Life and not question for one minute why we take the classes that we do, I can tell you that we will have completed the courses of learning to allow us to inherit a kingdom of eternal peace and joy. Now this may be a good starting point to tell you who you really are.

Let me tell you first who the world says you are. The world has changed a lot since I was a child. We still had a black and white TV at the farm and we spent a lot of time watching it in the evening. I remember my father watching the news which exposed him to global events while living in a very isolated rural community. Our television allowed us all to stay informed on the latest news. I remember the World of Disney - it was the highlight of the week for entertainment. We could also watch comical family shows like the Partridge Family and the Brady Bunch which portrayed the lighter side of family life. Of course, Star Trek was also a big hit that could take a child on a space voyage to another planet to experience all kinds of adventures. This type of thinking was a catalyst for the future which would create space programs and missions into space. Before anything was created temporally, it had a spiritual creation or an intuition that created a thought in the mind to work from. I don't recall the product commercials in detail, but remember most of them related to some functional use for the household. I'm sure there were liquid cleaner commercials, laundry detergent commercials and anything that was deemed a need for consumers. Well, our needs seem to have changed over the past forty years. And it is these commercial images that are defining who we are and what we need to be happy.

It seems that TV and media has become a double edged sword. Not only are we exposed to the latest and greatest of everything in life, but we also have TV therapist and talk show hosts that allow us to remedy the inherent needs that have developed through our social growth and learning. We can see an acceptable external dimension where beautiful men and women have been slated as parts in dramatic roles and ficticious lives to leave us believing that my life must be boring or unfulfilled without living this screenplay. We are bombarded with car commercials that show sleek sexy men and women designed to lure us into believing that by owning one of these vehicles we too can have the glamorous lives portrayed by those models. We have diet programs to assist you to become everything that you could ever imagine by having a defined and perfectly fit body. We are exposed to advertising that promotes more financing to allow us the luxuries of life on one hand and then other commercials that allow us to consolidate our debt into just one easy payment. Even though the family size seems to be reducing to one or two children (and in some cases no children) home sizes appear to keep getting larger. These massive dwellings create more space for couples to get lost in and also drop the connection that once existed from merely holding the other person's hand and looking into their eyes. We are building larger and a greater numbers of universities to attain professional degrees. It seems that everyone nowadays wants to become a lawyer or doctor. The advertising industry has tapped into the wave of baby boomers recognizing this generation as a goldmine of consumers. Targeting these individuals and offering whatever it takes to have for their money.

Now don't get me wrong, there are many worthy pursuits in life, but for right now I want to focus on who you are, rather than who you may want to become. The first reminder is the awakening that when you came into this life you had nothing but the mere physical body that the Divine Spirit and your parents created for you to embody your spiritual energy. Next, when you leave this life you will take with you nothing more than the matured spiritual energy and the body that your parents originally gave to you to house that spirit. So let's suppose first of all that this spirit which was created by a loving Source Energy intended you to have this experience and nothing more. I draw a parallel to the popular movie entitled, "*The Matrix*". The essence of the Hollywood blockbuster was a heroin named Neo, who was faced with the choice to either live in an existence of truth or in an existence of illusion. He chose by deciding to swallow either the red pill or the blue pill. The blue pill would allow Neo to continue living the life of illusion. The red pill transported the hero to reality. The Matrix was merely a visual illusion that an individual believed was real and the machine behind this delusion made sure that everyone continued to go through the motions of their lives without question. For those who chose not to believe in the Matrix – those who swallowed the red pill - they were able to see beyond the illusion and experience reality and the internal workings of human life on earth. They understood the true reality and believed in a greater cause. They were directed by oracles giving them messages to guide them along the path of their ultimate mission. Neo came to understand who he was and his assignment in life - to battle against the machine world and expose to all humankind, the illusion of life.

The movie was a brilliant portrayal of this worldly existence and the fact that there are two very different philosophies for human existence. I am humored by the part in the movie where one of Neo's colleagues betrays him for the tradeoff of being accepted back into the Matrix of illusion after having come to the truth. The look of pleasure in the betrayor's face as he bites into a juicy steak, making the comment of how much he missed the taste of this food, even though he knew that it was only an illusion. Illusions in life are so strong that while many people experience them and enjoy them, these apparent joys will eventually consume them and rob them of their true identity. Such false impressions will deny them the ability to see through the fantasy in order to understand who they really are and how they originally came to this earth. Respect for others in their pursuit of life is absolutely one of the rules that we all must follow. We can offer truth, but ultimately whether each person acts on this truth will be of their own free will and choice. The Source has not only given each person the gift of life, but also granted them choice - free agency, or the freedom to act on their knowledge of this existence. While each person has this liberty to act, they do not have the ability to control the outcomes. We will explore this concept in greater depth in the chapter devoted to our purpose.

Through the Hindu belief, I have learned many things about life and who we are. These truths have been repeated over and over again in other religions and philosophies as applied within the realm of their faith and I have come to accept them as a truth of understanding. There is only one truth that exists in this life. This truth is a law similar to the law of gravity and the law of entropy. We cannot change the fact that gravity exerts a force downward upon the planet at 3.81 m/s^2, nor can we oppose the law that systems which begin in an ordered state become disordered, and that this state can never be reversed under natural circumstances. These truths about life have manifested to me over and over, time and time again, and I have come to see them as very real and tangible. They have been an important tool in understanding who I am.

First, let us discuss the difference between Soul Consciousness and Body Consciousness. As I mentioned before, the ego which is an enemy to God, was first developed when we were small children. In children of divorce, this ego develops in an unhealthy way which manifests itself later in adult life. Ego was developed in a state of fear, shortage, disapproval and abuse that caused the child to believe there was a loss of control. Trauma was the basis of life for the child; the feeling of love and regard did not exist. Because they could not trust mommy and daddy to take care of them, the ego told the child, that it would do the job in place of their parents. The ego would teach the child how to feel better and to protect it from pain, anguish and disappointment. This protection would be by means of deceit and lies that would allow for a predicted outcome. In the belief of the ego, children will do anything as people-pleasers just to have a specific reward for their action. The child could not trust the parents to give them the security of the family, so the child would learn to get value and validation through other means. The field of feeding the ego and its incessant needs have grown ripe in this 21st century society that we live in.

I am talking about an unhealthy field of dreams. In other words, feed it (the ego) and it will take care of you. While Soul Consciousness is all about defining yourself as a spiritual being, Body Consciousness is all about the ego defining your existence in this life. The ego has told the adult child of divorce, that if they just go on to take care of themselves from a Body Conscious state, they will feel better and be empowered. Ego appears to help us rationalize our state of being so that we can endure through periods of when we are feeling disempowered, lost and confused. Let's face it, who wouldn't feel good about themselves if they had a million dollar home, drove a Mercedes, had a beautiful wife or companion, looked like a super model or movie star and a couple of million dollars in the bank. Body Consciousness defines who we are by appearance, financial wealth, material possessions and the elevated status of what we do for a living. The pursuit of excellence in ones life is an admirable goal but the underlying question is all about defining who you are. And by knowing who you truly are, would you be willing to give it all away tomorrow in the security of consciousness that these things, which have been acquired, do not define who you are and your intrinsic worth. Ego is clearly driving most people across North America and the Western World, and we have come to gauge our worth on the basis of how we are doing from a Body Conscious state. Children of divorce are on this Body Conscious treadmill ever pursuing this ultimate goal to feed their internal need for self worth and if they are not quite there, don't worry - there is another program out there to get you what you want. In the end, life turns out to be nothing more than a competition with yourself to acquire enough Body Conscious acquisitions to feel like you are a success in life. I am not trying to portray a pessimistic view here, nor the need to have the essentials for living and providing for a healthy family environment eliminated from your thinking. I am attempting to help you to understand the Matrix as it exists in reality and the incessant feeding of egos that occurs to individuals who have become subject to some type of deprivation in their childhood. It is this lack of knowledge in who they really are and what really matters that is driving them to define themselves in a Body Conscious manner. This motivation is in direct opposition to what God, our Source Energy and Creator, has outlined for us to learn. Remember what I said about ego. Ego is the direct opposite of God and where ego exists, God does not. God is a loving Father that will allow us to exercise our human agency to come to the knowledge of choosing Soul Consciousness over Body Consciousness - whether we will swallow the red pill or the blue pill in our own means and time. Unfortunately, some will learn this early in their lives, some come to it later, and some never learn of it at all. Experiencing the knowledge of truth and Soul Consciousness is what will graduate us from this mortal experience and help us to learn the ultimate eternal joy that can be attained, rather than the limited happiness available through Body Consciousness. The attainment of this knowledge is not any easy row to hoe as Neo came to experience after swallowing the red pill. I can only tell you that it will be worth it in your lives should you accept this challenge. Let's spend some time in the process of Soul Consciousness, now that you know what it is not.

Soul Consciousness is about everything that makes you alive and everything in the world that keeps you alive. This state of elevated consciousness allows you to understand what you were created from and your existence in an eternal state. It is the comprehension of where you came from before this mortal existence, why you have been embodied here on earth to gain experience within this theatre and where you are going after this life and for what purpose. I have already explained the pre-existent soul world where we lived as spiritual siblings in a family environment. Dr. Wayne Dyer in his book, *"The Power of Intention*" describes the seven faces of Intention as Beauty, Creativity, Kindness, Love, Unlimited Abundance, Ever Expanding and Receptivity. These characteristics are virtues that have been used to define our loving Source. In his book, Dr. Dyer describes how understanding these aspects of the Source energy can help us in our own lives to create the world in which we wish to manifest for ourselves. The key to this accomplishment is to be in the same mind set as the Source. There are many indications that we share this same source energy with all living creations. When I studied biochemistry in university, I had the opportunity to examine the concept of quantum energy and while I am not an expert able to describe a full understanding of contemporary research, I do know that science has come to recognize an atomic level. Essentially, the idea of associative electrons which are contained within an orbital space with outer electrons orbiting the nucleus of an atom in a specific pattern that can be used at this high energy state to bond with others. In essence, everything in life is held together by these electron forces. From the tissues in our bodies to the living trees in nature, to the air that we breathe, and the water that we drink, anything which has been derived from atoms is held together with electron forces and shared bonding. This scientific concept helps us understand how we can be part of the Source Energy - the motivating force for creation and life. This life force is part of each human being and shared with all of nature and all that surrounds us. When we are in a Soul Conscious state, we live in a world that defines our lives in this shared realization. When we are in a Body Conscious (Ego driven) state, we live in a world of separation, one which refuses to accept being part of a whole. Remember that God and ego cannot exist in the same realm. There is only one truth and God is that truth while ego deceives people to believe that it is truth. This artificial truth was developed in childhood where the Soul began to lose trust and develop the basis for falsehoods that would attempt to control and confuse us in our pursuit of happiness. This is the basis of the Matrix.

If we believed and accepted the true understanding about our association with the Source Power, then there would be no misunderstanding about our existence and very purpose for living. If we could realize the power that existed in us as a child of a Divine God, we would be unlimited in our capabilities for co-creation. I remember teaching one of my sons about this concept of creation and he replied that he would like to think of an ice cream cone and blink his eyes to make it appear. I laughed at his enthusiasm, but I explained two concepts that may prevent him from accomplishing this for immediate results. First, we have to understand that to be apart of and not separate from the Source means being of one mind, one heart and strength with God. There is a commonly known scripture from the Bible where Jesus was in continual pursuit of understanding his Father's will and acting in accordance. So before we begin to co-create our world, we must first ask the Source if this is what the Divine Spirit would have us do. This is why great spiritual leaders have surrendered themselves to the Source Energy upon complete realization of themselves and their association to God. This is also portrayed within the definition of Trinity - the Godhead is all of one in body and purpose. The other concept to remember is that of putting training wheels on a bicycle for a child, our loving Source has slowed our life down to manage our developmental process. It is believed that God created the earth in six days, and then rested on the seventh. We also know from scriptural study that one day in God's time is one thousand years in our human time. So can you now imagine a creative process that God sees in one day – it is what we would realize in a thousand years. Imagine what your city, the land and regional geography looked like 100 years ago let alone 1,000 years ago. There has been a tremendous amount of creation and development that has occurred over that period of time, but because of its relative speed, we do not see the instantaneous effects within the creative process. I assured my son that if he took the correct steps to make that ice cream cone happen, it would. In detail if he would: step one get out of bed to walk downstairs and get a cone out of the cupboard after he had created that thought in his mind; step two take the ice cream out of the freezer, grab the scoop into a nice round ball; step three, plop that scrumptious ice cream on top of the cone; step four, put everything back into its proper place; step five, walk up stairs to his bedroom and sit back down to where he had been when we were talking about his imaginary blinking of the eyes, he would be holding the product of his mind's creation. The meaning behind this discussion and example is that if you all of a sudden sped up that sequence by a time ratio of the number of seconds in one day as compared to the number of seconds in 1000 years, he would see the miraculous appearance of an ice cream cone – in an instant - as he desired. This is only one example of a creative process. Can you imagine the steps that led to the creation of a whole individual that enters into a bond with another to form a union, which will eventually produce offspring of similar like form? We have been given an opportunity to co-create with God and it is essential that we understand the destructive forces that exist and prevent this essential learning process.

Along with the seven faces of Intention, I would go further to say that we possess any virtue that one could ever imagine. In our limited mortal existence, we do not have the comprehensive ability to define who we are, or who God is because this definition is without end and ever expanding. There is no end to the good that we are, or the capability that we have. The only thing that limits us is our fear and the boundaries that we create for ourselves. When we see ourselves connected to a God that has no boundaries, we start to realize our own limitlessness as well. We can experience a life of unlimited thought, but we first have to let go of a life that has only limited thinking. Much like a baby learning to walk, who first grabs everything and anything to stand on its own, eventually learns the joy of freedom and unlimited mobility by releasing all fear and letting go to trust its inner self and the balance it has acquired – and a belief that this act is possible. In the Bible, Jesus tells us to become as little children. I believe he was talking about this process of letting go of all fears and the ego, to learn the truth by swallowing the red pill and taking that step of courage and faith.

Let's now take a walk out the front door of our home as a Soul Conscious human being, as compared to a Body Conscious human being. I wake up in the morning, go through my regular routine and walk out my door for another day in life. Upon leaving the doorway, I look up into the beautiful blue sky and think about the endless universe, and the significance of this planet called Earth that I live on playing a role within the realm of my existence. I realize that the tree that I just walked by contains the same living source energy as what is contained within me and I feel completely connected as my hand brushes the leaves that are waving to me in the wind. As I walk to the bus stop where I catch my commuter downtown to my office, I think of all the things that I must accomplish today and now reference them as creations yet to be performed. I am more careful to realize the long term effects of my thoughts and ideas considering that they could affect the lives of many other people that I am connected to within this great creation of life. The bus driver smiles at me and says good morning and now rather than see him as another ethnicity, classified in a specific job, I look at him as my spiritual brother whom I likely had contact with before I came to this mortal experience. I realize that because of God's creativity, He made us all different to appreciate the beauty and wonder of the human creation. He gave us diversity in culture and belief to gain appreciation for all living organisms in life. I have come to realize that because we are all one, if there is any need that I have for any purpose of creation, the Source Energy will provide all that is required as long as it is in sync with the overall plan for life. As I travel along the bus route, I see that each thing visible in my life was created to give me joy and for the learning and benefit of this life. I also realize that to be apart of the whole, I also have an obligation and responsibility to give back a part of myself to all of creation. I am a literal steward over my life, which includes my thoughts, actions, deeds and all relationships. My new understanding as a Soul carries me far beyond any worldly care of a Body Conscious nature. I realize I am not the job I do as a janitor in a hospital, I am not the bus I ride in to work, I am not the apartment I rent for my children and me, I am not the small savings that I accumulated in my bank account for the benefit of my children. I now realize that I am a child of God, who is a Supreme Source and Divine Soul who has an eternal inheritance for me in the life to come. I know that being a child of such an Omnipotent Being is of far greater worth than anything I could ever define in the realm of this limited lifetime. I realize that it is my responsibility to separate the real world from the unreal world, the spiritual realm from the unspiritual realm to realize the purpose of my existence. On this basis, I will experience the greatest love story of my life when I have truly realized who I am and shed all the definitions that the world has given me because of the role I accepted to play while in this drama of life.

Chapter 8: Why Am I Here?

Dear Children,

We've covered who you are, now we will shift to an understanding of why you are here. The next chapter called, "What is my purpose", is very close to the objective of this chapter, however, I am going to generalize the reason and understanding why we exist in this life and then in the next chapter, I will expand more fully on a purpose driven life. By bringing these two chapters together in thought, I hope that you will begin to understand that your life has a significant meaning, that coincidence does not happen and that your existence has a powerful purpose. The challenge is for you to understand what that purpose is, and I hope to help you find the pathway that will give you your own understanding for your life. Your existence is unique and there is no other life like it on the planet today. It is unlike any other life that has ever been since the beginning of time.

So let us begin with a review about the pre-existence. Your Creator, the Source Energy, took part of its energy, or let's call it intelligence, and used it to create you. You might ask yourself, why? The simple answer is that this loving Eternal Parent's intrinsic character is to be ever expanding and you are part of this extension. God can expand His spiritual energy and influence throughout space and eternity, so it is His mission to create more of Himself. In the Bible it says that we're created in God's image, both male and female. Genesis talks more about our temporal bodies and I will get to that, but understand that before there can be a temporal creation, a spiritual creation is required. As in life, before anything tangible is created or manufactured, there has to first be an inspiration, a thought. God created you by His very thought, that by you He would continue to fulfill His purpose to ever-expand His energy into eternity. This is far beyond the galaxies, universe or solar systems that we could ever imagine. As spiritual children of a God, just like infant children of this world, they are innocent, beautiful, loving and have all the characteristics of the parents that created them. In the physical sense, we are a product of both our parents' genome. This combination gave us different physiological characteristics however, there is a general pattern of two arms, two legs, your main body, etc. In the same way, you were also created in a sacred spiritual form that resembles our Divine Parents; however, each spiritual creation is unique because of the content. Here is an analogy that may help explain: like electrons share a common characteristic among all types of atoms, they also act in varying forms based on the shell in which they occupy and the energy level in which they exist. They also have varying orbitals in which to travel. God has created a very specific spiritual code just as the unique genetic code that is contained within the nucleus of each cell within your body. This same process occurs in all of God's creations including the world in which we live. This will be an important theme to remember when we begin to talk about our life within the world of existence.

Little children are completely pure and innocent. Many times throughout Jesus' life, he beckoned His people to become as little children. Children are an example in life to learn from. They come to us in a gentle and immaculate form to teach us about God. We have so much to learn from little children. Watch a small child grow and voice their hopes, dreams and aspirations. With a healthy base development and loving parents, I would say that 10 out of 10 times, a child wants to become just like their parent. I grew up living in the country on a farm, and my first inclination was to become a farmer just like my dad. In a similar way, as sacred children created by a Spiritual Energy Source, we existed with this creator and came to love them. We identified ourselves by this Omnipotent Power and knew that we were created from the very essence of this Source. The Spirit Source had characteristics and virtues that were endless. We lived in the security of a protected life as spiritual children until the point that we would be required to implement our essence of being. This would be called Life, as we so often refer to it. By the means of this life our theoretical knowledge would be put to the test.

We know that the Bible outlines the creation of earth and the steps God took to create it. Each step was a temporal evolution that occurred over thousands of years. I know that scientific carbon dating has shown the earth to be millions if not billions of years old, but rather than debate the issue, understand this in the realm of an Omnipotent Being. If God used spiritual matter, or intelligence, to create our spirits and it appeared to date us a few thousand years old, the dating would originate from the Source which would be millions or billions of years old - even an eternity. All I am saying is that we tend to get caught up in the semantics of the world and its creation within the confines and limitations of our thinking as a temporal being. But let's imagine that the temporal earth was created by matter that was billions of years old, but had been brought together in time, to date it back six thousand years, so one of God's days is 1,000 years in our existence. Can you imagine the changes that could take place in one thousand years? It seems to me that the Source took progressive steps in each creation along the way. First it was the earth matter that became organized, which scientists like to call, "The Big Bang Theory", and I am sure it was a very large bang when all that mass came together. Next it was the heavens, with the light and the darkness, and then it was the oceans and then the plants, next the earth received animals and then the last and final feat of creating human life, man and woman. What is so beautiful to me is that God named everything. Now how thoughtful is that, to make a statement that each temporal creation would be identified with a name much like your name is important to you. So let's go back to the thought about the spiritual creation of the world. Just as our sacred formation occurred, the spiritual creation of the earth and all upon it also occurred. Just as our physical bodies consist of organs, tissue and cellular matter that is broken down to molecules of atoms and electrons circulating to bond and act like glue to hold us together, the earth is held together by this bonding effect of a spiritual energy. We have a useful knowledge of something called a periodic table that has helped us to understand that all things are created from some element within this table and probably others that we have not yet discovered. Even the space that we cannot see with our eyes let alone the extent of its molecular form, we are able to put our hand out the window while driving our car and feel the oxygen diatomic molecules that push our hand in the wind.

Now take away all of the nuclei, excluding the electrons, in other words, look out into the world with the magnification of a microscope, then take away everything excluding the electrons. What you would see is the spiritual creation of your existence. I imagine a bright glowing light, but I have dimmed it down using filters so that I can see the spiritual outline of each creation. If I return the nuclei to the associated electrons, I am able to see the physical or temporal creation. Much like in the movie, "*The Matrix*", the ability to differentiate between these two views will be important for further understanding. Understand that all things were created for our growth and learning, and especially that all these things that were created arc good.

Since the beginning of time we know of a biblical story where Adam and Eve were created. They were created equal, both male and female and were commanded to multiply and replenish the earth. In other words, they were meant to have children. Can you imagine how far the earth would have gotten without their participation? Suffice to say, there wouldn't have been a whole lot of expansion going on. This same thing is also applied to all living organisms. Obviously, as with university, there is a time to graduate, a time for the final thesis to be written and then to allow more room for other spiritual children to come down to this existence. This cycle of life is integral in the limited timeframe we spend in a mortal existence. So God created both man and woman to be able to reproduce their own kind and to experience a mini-creation in the temporal sense. In one of the courses I studies at university, we explored the biology related to embryology – an absolutely fascinating subject. The complexity and cellular signaling through our genetic DNA only strengthens my belief in a greater power that is responsible for this orchestration of life as we know it. The first step was to be created spiritually, then a housing for this spiritual creation came next, after which, more creations would occur within the realm of each individual creation to continue to sustain life. There are many people who do not ever find a soul connection in order to enter a union where this procreation is possible, so let me say that even though this is an important aspect to life, it is not absolutely essential for everyone to experience if the given opportunity does not arise. I am not saying that you should try to avoid this learning experience if the opportunity does present itself. It's like when you are working towards a university degree, you have core courses that you must take but you also have some flexibility to gain further knowledge in other areas. These extra-curricular courses will give you a greater diversity of knowledge and expand your understanding on a variety of different topics. It would be helpful if some of the courses offered could help us understand how to have healthy relationships and spiritually healthy families. Those areas would be gaining experience of actually pro-creating another human being and second of all, creating a family unit of parents with their offspring. This would also create greater understanding of being a parent with a partner, and being responsible for teaching and nurturing children.

Now, this may start to sound a little familiar. We came from a family environment in the spiritual pre-existence, so we are just replicating temporally what was once created spiritually, not in its actual form with God as our father but in the sense that we are now in a temporal form - having created a family to parallel our experience from the pre-existence. This family would offer nurturing to the children that are brought into the world and it would also be the basis for all association to society. The family would produce the infrastructure in the world in which we live in. This family unit will prove to be the success or destruction for all of mankind. The family is the most important organization or unit that was ever created spiritually and temporally. The concern I have, is the destruction of this family unit and the overwhelming acceptance that our society has adapted to over time. I realize that there is a need to address contemporary issues that face the world today, but it is my objective to create an understanding that will either help children of divorce heal from the effects of a dysfunctional home or to assist parents to think about the long term effects of their decisions when considering separation of a family that will eventually end in a divorce. Better yet, let's understand the effects of divorce before we make commitments to long-term relationships that could result in the creation of children.

We know that our spiritual creation came down from the spirit world to join a temporal creation here on earth. The spiritually-created world gained a temporal structure that would be sustained by the pro-creation of the originating humans that brought it into the world. So if we want to become like our Creator, because we are in essence made from the Divine Spirit, what is it that we have to learn? We obviously have to learn how to create. This may seem basic when we compare the thought with creating a floral bouquet or a painting, but understand that a creation is a creation no matter how large or small it may seem. The steps are the same whether it is building a house for the first time or it is God creating the planet in which we now live. What we create may appear to be less significant because of our measured time and its relation to eternity. When we look at God's creation of the earth, we are mystified and impressed that such an event could occur. And yet, the Source Power has used the same principles that we use in our everyday lives and have become so naïve about the significance of it all. We are like little Harry Potters and Hermaites walking around in life with our magical wand experimenting with these God given powers to produce either happiness or pain within the realm of our own lives. If we can grasp the concept of how to create good things in our lives, we can go on to experience great joy and happiness much like the experience we had in our pre-existence. However, with the agency that God has given us, we can also create pain and sorrow if our creations do not follow the universal laws of Heaven. We are free to act for ourselves with this agency, however, we are not free to determine the associated consequences, for it is by these consequences that we also learn.

Every creation that has some sort of beginning, is influenced by all energy that is existent in the world. This energy is best described in David Hawkins work called, ***"Power vs. Force"***. Dr. Hawkins has concluded the significance of being able to measure some type of associated energy to every sensory stimulus within the world. So whether it is associated to thinking, activities, consumables, verbal, visual, audible, smell, touch, all have some sort of associated energy that will either strengthen or weaken the human consciousness. Every decision we make, or creation that we initiate, is on the basis of human consciousness. We know that all things that God created were good, but why is it then that we do not create all things good. Why do we have bad experiences or bad marriages? Why is it that we make bad decisions in our lives that create sadness and sorrow? Well, it is pretty much like the reason we can create a very bad tasting cake. If we do not put the right ingredients into it, we use too much sugar or flour or starch, we will experience a distasteful product. Fortunately, many creations that we experiment with do not have an over-riding impact on our lives, nor do they create any long term affects that can be a resultant chain reactive dysfunction. Unfortunately, this cannot be said of children that were created into homes of divorce. It seems that most creations in life can develop a recovery strategy, and because I have experience being an adult child of divorce and the inherent malfunctions, I hope to not only stress the significance of the family unit, but also emphasize how you might avoid this very problem by understanding the effects of separation.

Let's first discuss creations more in-depth and what influences affect them. So the question to ask ourselves is - are we creating a good life or a bad life? Are we creating a good career path or a bad career path? Are we creating good friends or bad friends? Are we creating good thoughts or bad thoughts? Are we creating good relationships or bad relationships? So the overall, life-challenging question is - are we creating good families or are we creating bad families that can inherently create functional or dysfunctional children from that family. Well society says that we are what we eat, or more importantly, what we wear, which directly correlates to the ego that says that we are what we look like, how much money we have, what our status is or what we do for a living, or possibly how big our home is or what kind of car we drive. This is a lie according to what our understanding is from a spiritual realm. This is the ego talking. That's right, the ego that is the enemy to God. This is the same ego that was developed in a child to protect itself from the harm or the world that associated itself with fear. Remember this ego, the one that lies, cheats, controls, steals and mistrusts in times of any conflict. My ego was developed in being a child of divorce and feeling abandoned and rejected at a very early age. The child in all people desires to feel love and regard. We will always have that child present within us, according to Dr. Caroline Myss as she writes in her book, *"Sacred Contracts"*, the important thing to recognize is that this child has grown into an adult. Depending on how much power you give to that child, will determine how that child may respond in adult life. If as a child you lied and people-pleased to avoid conflict in order to have an outcome of peace in the home, chances are if those same circumstances present themselves within the realm of the adult life, you will display the same self-preservation techniques. Because the adult is trying to avoid abandonment and rejection within the realm of conflict in a relationship, possibly a marriage, the adult will resort to the survival techniques developed as a child to be spared the feared outcome. This is why the act of one spouse threatening the other that they will divorce is such a damaging factor. Not only is this threat creating fear in the adult child of divorce, but it is projecting low energy that is causing fear, anxiety and withdrawal. Because of this low energy attractor, it will go on to attract other low energy activities. Possibly, it will cause the spouse to go out and get excessively drunk, or use drugs, or engage in acts of violence, or have an affair outside the marriage in an act of betrayal. On the other hand, if individuals are fully aware of the effects of low energy influence and try to resolve issues on the basis of high energy thinking of trust, courage, acceptance, forgiveness and love, then the actions will attract other positive attractors for a more positive outcome. In the case of an adult child of divorce, which there are so many of these people like you and me, there needs to be an understanding that this ego developed in a dysfunctional divorced home where love and regard was not nurtured. What occurred was ego development inherent to the break down – and the result is damage to the child and the future adult's character will manifest over and over again unless the issue is addressed. So let's generally say that bad things are created when associating ourselves with negative energy, and that it attracts more negative energy. This could be visible by people who are experiencing a downward spiraling in their lives, possibly never pulling out before they hit rock bottom. This is not the healthy airplane ride that climbs and descends. This descending dive is to be avoided at all costs. Pilots refer to it as the graveyard spiral and for good reason.

The antithesis of this association to negative attractors is the essence of the Source Energy's existence and its virtues. If God is defined by Beauty, Creativity, Kindness, Love, Unlimited Abundance, Ever-Expanding and Receptivity, just on those virtues alone, our creative forces would go a long way. Everything that we create is based on these seven virtues and when we align our creative thought with that of the Divine Source Energy, it offers us the kind of results that we are looking for in life. We are given many opportunities to create on a very small scale, but when it comes to making major long-term decisions that will affect our lives significantly; we need to understand that only when we are in tune with our Divine Maker will we understand what creations have potential for long-lasting happiness in our lives. This most important creation would be initiated with whom we choose to marry or make a life time commitment to. This person, ideally, would embrace equal values and concepts on creation and respect the institution of that union and its pro-creative potential.

There is a scripture that says, "What God brings together, let no man put asunder". This passage emphasizes that if our minds and hearts are one with God in our creative efforts, we will be successful at making daily choices that will give us a positive and constructive process in motion. This is the only way to joy and happiness. By following truth which leads us to make good choices, the Source Power slows our lives down significantly in order to have a lot of time to experiment with this concept. We are given more time to think about decisions that we make and their consequences. He gives us a specific rate of physiological development that takes us through the various stages of our lives when different things have more importance than others. Obviously, at the age of 16, we are more concerned about creating enough money to buy our first car than we are thinking about marriage and having children. We may eventually get around to thinking about marriage or a life partner however, depending on what has occurred in our lives up until that point and what types of energy we have associated with during our developmental years, the sound and level-headed thinking we may apply to this important decision may vary. It depends on what kind of energy we continue to associate ourselves with. We will make decisions or perform creations with our Harry Potter wand much to our happiness or dismay depending on what we have understood of the creative process.

As spiritual children we not only have the responsibility to live good lives but we also must learn to acknowledge the Source Power every day for giving us the opportunity to enter this school of life. This is where we will get more into the

Matrix of making a decision to swallow the red pill. In the Hindu belief, there is an understanding that in opposition to the Supreme Spirit, the character of Maya is continually appearing to deceive each soul so that it may be influenced more by its vices, rather than to be drawn to the virtues of our Divine Creator. Let's consider again how these vices can affect our lives and divert us from why we are here.

The vices are anger, greed, lust, ego and attachment. As noted previously, all of these characteristics of consciousness appear around the logarithmic values of 100-175 on Dr. Hawkin's map of consciousness. So not only are they counterproductive in the creative process, but they are misleading and attractors to more negative energy. Not only do these vices oppose the Source's energy, they are detracting and pulling one to be out of harmony and disconnected with the Supreme Soul. And when we are not in one mind with this Creative Force, we are most likely in a mode of destruction. I'm sure that this is the main reason why Hindu's believe in a need, as many other religions, to acknowledge God always whether it is in their daily prayers, meditations, church meetings, family life or through each person's thoughts, deeds and actions. If we associate with Maya's characteristics, there is a great danger of creating the wrong thought, which is the precursor to the wrong choice which will ultimately produce the wrong creation. The main reason that Maya is so successful at drawing attention to the invitation of vices, is because they are directly associated to living a Body Conscious lifestyle as compared to a Soul Conscious lifestyle. Going back and reviewing what we discussed about Body Consciousness, it is about defining who you are by what you look like, how much money you have, what your status in society is, your educational accomplishments, how big your home is or what kind of car you drive. These are thoughts of comparison that often draw anger, when we have not achieved what others may have. Such thoughts give rise to a lust of taking, rather than an attitude of giving, greed or longing to acquire more possessions rather than being happy for the life that you have. An attachment gives you false security that would totally devastate you if you were to lose everything tomorrow. An ego will define you by Body Consciousness elements of success and will provide that sense of achievement at whatever cost of loss to others it may afford. Doesn't sound too pretty does it? That's because it's not. And yet, people in the temporal world continue to prey upon the ego and drive their desires towards greater materialism. The question comes right down to whether we can put off the natural man/woman who is living in the Matrix or temporal view of life - and put on the spiritual man/woman and take the red pill to see the real meaning and purpose as to why we exist on this planet we call earth. Let us continue our discussion about purpose and finding purpose in our lives.

Chapter 9: What Is My Purpose?

Dear Children,

Life teaches us about our purpose and who we are over a period of time. Obviously, at birth, when we are an innocent child coming into the world, the last thing that we think about is what is our purpose? This little baby is manifesting the purest form of our purpose without even knowing it. There is a scriptural reading that says, "Men are, that they might have joy" and of course, this also applies to women. I don't think I have ever seen the manifestation of this in any purer form than looking at a little baby smiling, cooing, batting its eyes and emanating an absolute pure form of love and peace from its very being. If we stop and consider that this creation has recently arrived on Heavenly Flight 101, we would recognize that this spiritual form, which has just received its temporal form of being, has yet to be tainted by any low energy that exists in the world today. This is based on the fact that its mother has recognized the importance of not associating with any form of negative attractors or low energy stimuli. This is why it is so disappointing to see an expectant mother puffing on a cigarette or drinking alcohol or putting any type of harmful substance into their body, because this ultimately will affect the developing fetus. It is widely known that smoking while pregnant can constrict the umbilical cord. So what makes a person do this? This could very well be a person struggling with the vices that were developed in their childhood from some dysfunctional environment. Only through understanding and applying effective principles, can these inherently developed vices be overcome.

So we know that our purpose is not completely revealed right from the beginning. We know that from scriptural account, even Jesus did not completely understand his mission in life, only that he was meant to understand and then act on this. I am sure Moses also had no idea of his purpose and mission in life - even after the God of Israel appeared to him and commanded him to lead the Israelites out of the land of Egypt. Moses still resisted his calling on the basis that he did not feel that he was capable of this task. It is essential for a parent to envision the purpose of the child they are raising. We cannot always understand the mission in life our children will have or what kind of career or interests they will choose for themselves. However, given the understanding and knowledge of our Divine Spiritual Creation and initial Spiritual Family origin, that awareness can assist a child to not only develop in a healthy high energy form, but also recognize talents and capabilities that seem to be part of their character. Such God-given characteristics can direct that child in ways that they can then appreciate their distinctive individuality. This is why the effects of a damaging dysfunctional family can be significant in relation to long term effects in a child's life.

The best gift that a parent can give to their child is a temporal existence which imitates the existence that they originally came from. We must learn the very essence of who we are before we can know the purpose of our lives. Everyday, whether we are teaching our children or recognizing this for the first time in our lives as an adult, when we realize who our Divine Source Parent is, we begin to recognize our very nature as well. We begin to see beauty in our soul as well as our temporal creation and know that God loves us and we are good, because everything that He created was and is good. We need to see beauty in other people and all creations in life, rather than judging or taking for granted the splendor of a crimson red sunset that is painted across a blue sky or the perfection in the pattern of petals within a single rose. We need to understand that these magnificent creations that we are able to experience are who God is, and the immaculate nature within God.

Think of the simplicity in the words of our Creator as He speaks in a literal sense of defining who He is when He says, "I am, who I am". Can our Source Energy and Creator make it any more plain than that? He is everything that ever exists that is good, because we know that good means God. It is also important to know that God is kind. Tender mercies are evident in our life every day. We often see many kind acts that people do for others. I know in my own life when I have been kind to another being or creation, my heart bubbles out in joy for the connection that was made. We must learn how to love each other and the central characteristic of giving rather than the lust-based act of taking. The world seems to be very confused about love, primarily because we have only one word to define such a large concept. In the Greek language, the meaning of eros, philia and agape all mean love but each describe a different kind of love. Eros is the kind of love that draws you into a chemical attraction to another being that could stimulate the pheromones of a species attracting a mate for union. Philia is love which is derived in our hearts on the basis of loving another because of the brotherly or sisterly connection that is felt aside from any other feeling or motivation. Agape is the kind of love that God portrays in His unconditional love for each of his creations. When we love another and are able to accept them without any conditions, and are able to forgive any shortcomings, then this is agape. Love is always about giving, it is not about taking. When you love, you are more concerned about the other person than you are about yourself. You want more for others than you want for yourself. In every act of love, we need to ask ourselves deep within, do we want more for the other person than we want for ourselves? If we are acting out of selfish motivation where we have a hidden agenda to get something in return for our efforts, this is not a true act of love. Lust is all about taking or ensuring that we satisfy ourselves which may be at the cost of others. Lust is a vice of Maya and is to be avoided at all costs. This desire is derived out of low energy and will only pull you down towards other negative attractors that will leave you feeling empty and without purpose. We need to learn that we have creative capabilities within our power to design any type of life that we desire. We know that God is creative. We know that we are derived from God, so we then know that we are also creative. In many senses, creativity is manifested through all aspects of living. We know that God is good, so as His spiritual children, he also wants us to create all things that are good. It is unfortunate to know that sometimes, to know the good, we must experience the bad. I am not saying that learning to be like God is always going to give us a positive experience, but it will give us experience to help us understand what is good, and what it would be like to create good in our own lives because of this understanding. When we conceive, we also need to understand that there is abundance in life and no limitations. Only we are capable of limiting ourselves, which is generally on the basis of what we have come to believe, as it has been taught to us by our parents. Some parents don't teach us anything about who we are, so I hope this book may be a resource to you. That you may grasp the wherewithal available to you and the abundance our Source Creator offers you. Your access is unlimited and you are only held back by your limited thinking. There is a saying that goes, "Whatever the mind can conceive and believe - it will achieve." So until we understand who we really are rather than being defined by limited body conscious awareness portrayed in this temporal life, we will continue to be unaware what our boundless capabilities are. By knowing that God is ever expanding you will know that there really is no limitation to your capabilities. Unfortunately, we tend to draw a box around our lives and live within those confines. This box is generally a definition of what we have experienced in life up until that point. The longer we live, the more it seems that the walls around this box get higher. This imprinting makes us believe that our lives are limited and generally we never risk going beyond the boundary we set for ourselves. This concept is illustrated well in the movie called, "The Village". It's about a community of people that experienced trauma and became afraid to live in the regular confines of life. The initial pioneers that suffered this trauma set out to build a town that was isolated from regular life, and it would protect them from the evils that they were trying to avoid. Children were born, and families were raised within this village, and they were led to believe that some evil forces existed in the woods surrounding the village and nobody was allowed to leave. Those who were indoctrinated in this way of thinking believed in this fear of leaving the borders of the village. Even though tempted to explore, there was great apprehension about going beyond the confines that had been set. And so it is in our lives. We are led to believe that we need to fear what is beyond the realm of our own knowledge or our existence. As we are able to appreciate a God that has no borders and is not confined to the same space, but is ever expanding, we too will begin to realize the full potential of our being and existence. When we develop that understanding, we can then have courage to think in an unlimited manner so we may enlarge our world and experience as well as influence the lives of other people we were meant to interact with and have in our drama. All of this would have no meaning unless we were receptive to our Supreme Creator and His will for us. God is accessible to all of his creations both large and small. We know from the

Bible that even the flowers of the field are cared for by God. So how much more do we think that a loving parent will be receptive to the needs of his spiritual child? All of a sudden, "ask and you shall receive", has much more meaning when the asking is in harmony with this Source Energy. Then what was previously thought of as impossible becomes possible. Be receptive to your surroundings and other people. Understand they have been placed in your life for a purpose. When we begin to see that there are no coincidences in life and that all people, events and experiences were meant for a reason, then we begin to understand our very purpose for life. The crowning joy for existence is to identify your reason for living. This has nothing to do with money, status, appearance or any kind of material wealth and acquisition.

Let me tell you how I came to the knowledge of my purpose. I was sitting in a service center waiting to pick up my vehicle after getting it repaired and was watching the Oprah Winfrey show on the television placed in the waiting room. The topic that she was exploring in her talk show was about people who had found purpose in their lives. She talked to a variety of individuals. These were folks who had professional careers and at some point, came to an understanding that there was a deeper calling to their lives. I remember there were some people with an inspiration to teach children who were less fortunate than mainstream American students. The stories these individuals shared were truly inspiring. That program made an impression upon me which would manifest major changes later in my life. I returned to Canada after living in the United States for a period of four years. I had secured a position with a biomedical company in San Diego and I enjoyed the work immensely. But I was separated from my children who were living in Canada. And after going through yet another relationship loss, I felt the drive to return soon after the tragedy of 911. I realize the importance of my children in my life, and I knew that if I made them a priority by having a relationship, I would be able to put my career in motion and start all over again. After living in Canada two years, I still had not connected with any real certainty on a career, even though I seemed to be making some progress with having a relationship with my children. The industries that I had worked in during my previous years were either non-existent or it had been so long ago since I was in that line of work I was now disconnected from any meaningful contacts. I went through a job layoff and then another relationship separation, which left me feeling very distant from any type of purpose or even a drive for life. I kept searching for answers regarding a career and received an inclination about starting a consulting company. Long before that however, I had also received an inspiration regarding writing a book. The relationship breakdown hit me very hard because of the connection that that I felt for yet another person I had fallen in love with. I was emotionally battered and feeling a loss once again. The ending however propelled me into a recovery mode that would take me back to my childhood to investigate the effects of growing up in a home of divorce. The understanding opened up like a floodgate of knowledge. I became increasingly aware of the effects of divorce and how they had manifested in me, in my marriages and in other relationships. It was the first encounter in coming to a full understanding of the ego and how I had developed these unhealthy survival skills to attempt to control the outcomes of life. I started to realize that where we have come from, and the experiences we have had, all contribute to who we are and our very purpose in life.

I began to realize that rather than looking forward for some type of purpose, our objective would lie in looking back at where we came from. This method is also used when trying to predict future experimental data. I began to look at my past and plot every event, learning experience and situation that had ever happened to me like a cluster of scientific results. If my life had gone exactly how it was supposed to go, and there are no accidental events or occurances, then, what could I learn from where I had been in the past so that I could apply it to the future? Similar to how a scientist would look at information and see the trend of clustered data points, I also looked at this trend from the time that I was born and drew a line through the data points that would represent some trend for the future. Once I extrapolated this line, I realized that what I had been trying to create for my future was not consistent with the data of the past. I realized that the inclinations that I had been receiving from my Source Creator was more in tune with what I was to be doing in the future, rather than what my ego was driving me to do. I didn't tell anyone about this propensity because I believed they would have thought I had lost my mind, and that I would be the subject of others' ego-centric criticism. Such backlash would discourage me to the point where I would just go back to my ego driven purpose.

So I decided to write a book about my experiences, that I might give it to my children. My hope was that they would gain knowledge from my life experiences in order to have more successful lives and relationships; to have a greater amount of success and happiness with this understanding. The book would explain how I survived being a child of divorce, what inherent characteristics I developed as a result of this experience and how it had contributed to the destruction of my marital relationships. It would also outline the knowledge that I had acquired along the way that would give me the ability to heal from the devastating effects of this modern day plague that is affecting so many people today.

When I began my first day of writing I knew that this was what I was supposed to be doing. I had no idea how I would pay the bills. All I knew was that I would be following a prompting that had come from God and I could not deny it. Everything about it seemed so irresponsible and irrational in comparison to what constituted being a responsible adult at this time of my life. Many fears entered my thoughts – even a feeling of inadequacy. Feelings of doubt left me sensing that this task that I had undertaken was not practical and seemed somewhat ludicrous. I knew though that I had experienced an epiphany about what I should do in my life. It didn't necessarily make much sense, in the temporal world driven by ego. But I knew that if I was going to believe in my Source of Intention, and make it my purpose to appreciate and express the genius that I am, then I had to stop believing my ego and start believing the Creator from which I emanated to come to this life. It was a huge leap of faith for me. I was convinced that if my experience could save my children and help them to understand the effects of divorce, and what they needed to know could bring them success and happiness in life, then I was going to believe in Intention over my ego. I tried to not make it more than what my objective was, but I couldn't help thinking about other children who also suffered the effects of divorce, losses of a parent and other familial dysfunctions. Those who were now adults and who were trying to have relationships but failing each time, just as I had. There are so many adult children of divorce experiencing second, third and fourth marital relationship failures. Like me, these people would continue to spiral downwards into a feeling of hopelessness and despair. Some would even consider doing something drastic by ending their lives as my brother had done. All I knew was that I was now a man with a mission, to save my children and anyone else that would listen because I understood that the knowledge I had acquired and survived to talk about, would be the essence for healing many souls that were lost and looking for answers. These answers I now realized had come from my Divine Creator and I was to be the messenger to offer the way out, to heal and restore what was lost, to give hope and a reminder of why it is that we are actually here in this life and what it is that we are supposed to learn.

If this could all make sense, and we could live healthy and purpose-filled lives, then what would be our life after this earthly existence and what would our purpose be there? The next step in our journey is to explore the continuation of our existence into the next life.

Chapter 10: What's Next? Graduation!

Dear Children,

Like an earthly university, the time spent would seem somewhat wasted without receiving that little piece of paper at the end of your studies - the parchment that signifies you have met all the requirements for attaining that specific degree. That document announces to the world that you have completed a related study and now are able to offer your acquired specialty to a form of employment or profession. In some cases, students even choose to go on to do more post-graduate work in the area they specialize in. Generally, in some form or another, this knowledge begins to be applied in a real life scenario. What would be the point of just learning a whole lot of theory and never applying it to anything in life? I think this concept is outlined best by Stephen R. Covey in the *"Seven Habits of Highly Effective People"*. In this popular book Dr. Covey teaches that the way to sharpen the saw is to teach what you know to others. This coincides with applying the theory to our own life otherwise we have not fully become committed to this new knowledge. Life offers us the opportunity to learn a great deal of theory. We will even be given occasions to practice this theory in real life scenarios within the laboratory of every day living. All of this learning culminates into being specialized, and with this specialty, the Divine Spirit will give us many prospects to apply this learning and knowledge in the life to come. Before we go any further, let's look back and review the overall infrastructure that our Source Energy has provided for us. It's essential to clearly understand the realm of this world and complete the studied material in order to graduate prior to moving into our next responsibility.

The first thing we talked about was our spiritual existence prior to this life. We lived with our Divine Parentage which prepared us for a mortal life. This was the beginning of our spiritual identity and an understanding of our association with a Supreme Being that would initiate our temporal life from spiritual matter that we call intelligence. It is critical to recognize that sacred existence was essential to help us develop into beings that could recognize who we really are. Our full identity was created spiritually before this mortal existence, however, it was important for our memory to be limited for a variety of reasons. First of all, if we had a complete memory of this spiritual existence, we would not be able to develop in a temporal sense. If the moment that we entered this world, we had a complete memory of our spiritual origin, there would be no motivation to search for meaning and the true identity of who we are. This quest is part of the temporal creative process.

As we live in this temporal world, we discover hidden clues as to who we really are and our purpose for living. It's kind of like being on a scavenger hunt. I used to enjoy such adventurous play when I was a child. The game began when you were given a list of clues that would lead you to the treasure. From there you raced against the other players to identify all the clues, and bring the tangible treasure back to the finish line. In life, each spiritual creation has its own personal scavenger hunt. Individuals may cross over in commonality with other spiritual creations, but each life has a specific path that will be taken to reveal the understanding required for a future purpose.

We talked about attaining a temporal body for existence in this physical world. This body is a miraculous development. It started out as a mere microscopic pinpoint and developed into a full functioning living being - a product of contributing genetic material from both male and female parent. This body houses the spiritual form to allow it to experience a temporal life. Such a life includes growing through various stages of development physically, emotionally, intellectually and spiritually until the time of physical death which is simply another transition back to our spiritual existence. Physical development is predicted within the genetic material of our genome. What we look like, the rate at which we grow, whether we are tall or short, large or small is to a great extent predicted within an organized DNA system for physical development. We do have responsibility for how we take care of this structure by what we eat and how we respect it by giving it exercise and the way in which we treat it, but overall, the physical body will continue on a set path of development. Intellectual development begins from the time we are born into this world as a result of what our sensory organs connect with based on the type of experience we are able to have. To a great extent, our parents are responsible for our early exposure to stimuli for our intellectual growth especially as infants and toddlers. This is why parents have such a great responsibility to assist their children in learning and directing them during their early stages of development. Contemporary psychological studies are prompting parents to expose their children to a variety of stimuli at a very early age. When a child is able to experience with all senses, the world in which they live, the life of that child is uniquely benefited from this contact in the physical world because it gives it a sense of meaning and a feeling of oneness. Of course, development continues throughout our whole life as we take greater responsibility for our continued intellectual development by creating experiences and learning opportunities over our lifetime. Emotional development is greatly dependent on the experience that we have in this temporal life and is closely connected to several aspects of spiritual development. Outcomes from our experiences will greatly influence our lives and our thinking which will be directly associated with our ability to choose activities that are high or low energy producing. We will have a different understanding for each activity that we experience, and a culmination of knowledge will be attained by these occurrences. The resultant understanding will be stored in our long term memory and we will revert back to this again and again, throughout our lives. It is critically important to understand the responsibility the parent has to the child and also to comprehend the potential effects that a dysfunctional family can have on the child's life. If the development of a child is fully understood, then characteristics that the child may have developed as a result of a broken family unit may be addressed and corrected. For parents, this will offer new understanding to promote better direction for their own parenting skills.

Within the realm of life, you will make choices based on opportunities that are presented. Some choices will be significant and some will be unimportantly small and appear to have little or no affect. Each choice will be a chance for innovation and will follow a pattern based on a cognitive thought. It will be a mental or spiritual creation that has the potential for temporal creation by our own initiative. This initiative, which can start out as a drawing or written plan, can gain momentum based on the amount of commitment made. We all have ideas about what we would like to accomplish in life, but it is not only the creation of this idea but how well we follow the steps to implement it, that it may become a temporal creation. I could have a great plan for a house that I would like to build, and actually sketch it out on a piece of paper, but if I don't commit to it with a technical drawing, or arrange for financing or some other mode of payment, I will not actualize what I initiated. Each creation from start to finish has a developmental order, to which each is required to follow. If these steps are incomplete or missed in any way, the creation will also be lacking or incomplete in one way or another. To fail at learning the correct steps towards a healthy relationship, with proper dating and courtship, or by shortcutting the developmental process, will lead to inherent problems within this creation. And should this already flawed relationship continue to a full scale commitment of marriage, most assuredly, there will be serious problems. Once this miscreation is initiated, the challenges that prevail within the relationship of the husband and wife, will be further intensified in the subsequent family unit that may lead to having children. And all of this may unfold as a result of the misdirected steps of this relationship creation, from the very beginning. Therefore, making good choices, and following proper steps completely, will be a key to having and creating temporal results that will produce long term happiness and fulfillment.

The choices we make in life are influenced by the physical, emotional, intellectual and spiritual development that we experience. Something that is common to all of these aspects of development is truth. Truth is a powerful concept because when you understand truth, you also understand consequences. I like to think of this in the realm of universal laws. One example of this is the Law of Gravity. We understand the truth of this law by knowing that while on this earth, the law of gravity remains consistent in an open atmospheric condition. If I throw a ball off the top of a tall building, I know, based on the truth of this law, that it will accelerate downward at a rate of 3.281 m/s$^{\wedge 2}$ until it hits the ground which acts as a force pushing upwards to equalize the force that it creates when it falls. This truth is something that will not change and has been used by mankind to accomplish many great things. Gravity was an essential principle in order for scientist to understand how to propel rockets into space to explore our solar system. If scientists had not been successful at understanding and implementing this law into their choices, they could not have experienced success in the development of their creations. This is why understanding truth is so critical to our personal development and success in life. Truth is everywhere and obtainable in many different forms. I have seen truth in formal religions, as well as in university science textbooks. I have also experienced truth in thoughts that have come to my mind while simply looking at a painting. I have learned truth through individual experiences that I have obtained. So how do we understand the correct path for learning truth? For as many different people who exist in the world, there are probably as many if not more ways to find truth. Each spiritual child that comes to this temporal existence will find truth through their own efforts, desires and inspirations. The studies of Dr. David Hawkins in his book entitled *"Power vs. Force"* explains this journey another way. Whenever we experience some type of stimulus in life, it can either have a weakening or strengthening effect on our physical bodies. This has been measured through kinesiology and documented in Dr. Hawkins table entitled, "Map of Consciousness" as was mentioned previously. Everything that we experience in this life whether it is something we see, eat, hear, touch or verbalize has some associated effect upon our consciousness and whether we are weakened or strengthened by it. One of the more important aspects however, is the potential for this weakening or strengthening to attract more positive or negative consciousness. One example is smoking cigarettes. In the 1950's, smoking was not only socially accepted but looked at as an enjoyment and even empowerment in life. Through scientific research and medical technology, we now understand the deleterious effects of putting carcinogens into our body. Many people are dying or experience lung disease and other ailments because of this activity. Luckily smoking has decreased, however about 20% of the populace in North America still choose to participate. By acknowledging the truth that smoking is harmful, we are now able to make better choices based on this truth and subsequently most of us can enjoy better health. In Dr. David Hawkin's book, "Power vs Force", a kinesiological experiment was conducted that demonstrated the effect of simply holding a pack of cigarettes in one's hand can quickly show the weakening effects of this cancer causing agent.

Knowing the difference between truth and non-truth can make a big difference in our lives when we are experimenting with our creative capabilities. Understanding proven laws and scientific fact is one method you may use to understand truth. Another method that we more often associate in our search for truth is shear experimentation through trial and error. The problem with this however, is that there is so many influences in the world regarding what is right and what is wrong. There are differing values and goals that people are motivated by, but we do not see the results of these influences until they have had time to manifest themselves. We can see the attraction of buying the big house, driving the expensive cars and playing with the many toys, but we may not necessarily see the resultant bankruptcy for mismanagement of money, or the criminal conviction for theft in acquisition of these goods.

In general, we do not see the creative steps that others have taken, only the end result, therefore, somewhat of an illusion can exist when it comes to seeking truth, then using it in the creative process.

Part of what I have recognized from Dr. Hawkins map of consciousness is that when associating with low energy attractors, or what I would call non-truth sensory, there is also an emotional response of shame, guilt, apathy, grief, fear, desire, anger and pride. It is interesting to note that these emotions are also the Hindu vices which a spiritual student is advised to avoid. Other religious-based organizations also seem to have a moral or value code that guides their believer to avoid the types of activities that will produce these emotional responses. In general then, any activity that makes you feel bad or emotionally drained and weak is an activity to be avoided. I would suggest that this is a relatively good indicator of being associated with a non-truth. On the other hand, if an activity produces feelings of courage, trust, willingness, acceptance, reason, love, joy, peace and enlightenment, I would suggest that these type of emotions are produced and associate with positive attractors, and more likely to be connected with truth. Embracing these types of activities or sensory related stimuli will attract more similar energy and will result in leading a person on a correct pathway for finding truth. By understanding our feelings and emotional response to various experiences in life, we can start to differentiate activities that will bring us greater enlightenment. Such an understanding will lead us to make better choices during our creative education while upon this earth.

So, our goal is to learn how to make good choices in our lives. What kind of choices will we make? What sport will I learn? Who will be my friend? Where will I go to school? What will be my area of study? Who will I marry or will I get married? Will I have children and what kind of a parent will I be? The decisions we make in this life will be endless, both large and small, but one thing is for certain. Every choice will have some impact on our lives and the direction that we are headed, as well as with what speed. I believe that bad choices act as resistance in our lives. They tend to stray us from the course of truth and impede our originating route. Not that I am certain that we have a predesigned path, however, poor choices can create setbacks in our lives and we then have to learn how to deal with these. If we do everything to avoid setbacks and minimize the resistance, we can set our sail to direct our course on a surer heading for the learning that we are seeking to acquire.

In summary, you have gained a temporal body to house your spiritual creation to accomplish many aspects of life. This would include gaining an understanding of truth and non-truth, by differentiating between high energy and low energy experiences, learning how to create responsibly, gaining an understanding of who you are and what your purpose in life is. You can use your internal power to direct your life and to enjoy this life experience. This effort is similar to any endurance, just as one endures through the effort of any discipline to eventually graduate with knowledge unattainable anywhere else but in life. So what could we possibly do with all this knowledge and experience that we are acquiring?

We leave this temporal creation in the same manner that we came, only that we have different knowledge associated to the event. When we come to this life, there is celebration and a feeling of excitement for this new little being that has just arrived. We are full of wonder and amazement at the coming of this newly-created being, and we rejoice in the crowning of our creative powers. The creation of another human being and making possible for their existence in this temporal world is likely one of the most joyous events ever experienced. However, not all creative events are created equal. Not all preparations, economic or social conditions are the same. However, each soul is intended to this earth by its parents and the Source Power that made this entire learning experience possible. When we pass on to the next life, our spiritual creation is merely returning back to the presence of its Creator. The props, actors and worldly acquisitions are left behind only as a distant memory to our earthly existence. Remember why we came here in the first place. We were created as spiritual children and we are becoming aware of our association with our Divine Spirit, and our ultimate aim is to become like this Source. Remember that along with being kind, loving, beautiful, receptive, abundant and creative our Source Energy is also ever expanding. The possibilities with God are endless and when we are one with the Supreme Soul, our possibilities are endless as well. So think about this ever increasing nature of God and how we will apply it in the next existence.

It is difficult to talk about the next life because of our finite minds and the limited way in which we have become accustomed to thinking. Can you imagine though, a life that is unlimited or eternal in its realm? Think about a life with endless possibilities and opportunities for growth and understanding. I start to better understand eternity when I begin to think about who I am, not only in the spiritual sense but also in the temporal. Since the discovery of DNA and embryo development came to our understanding, our society has been on an even greater search to identify who they are and where they came from. We begin to realize that the genetic combination that we are developed from was derived from DNA that existed in our ancestors thousands of years ago. And this unique sequence has recombined many times over and over again since the very beginning. If we believe that our existence began from the creation of Adam and Eve, our parents that were first designed by God to live on this planet, then we can begin to realize that our temporal body, in which our spiritual creation is housed, has evolved through the recombination of DNA over thousands of years. The population of 6 billion people on the planet has grown significantly over the last 6,000 years and shall continue to grow through the children that the Spirit Source places on this earth. Nevertheless, whether you have children or not, and some people do not have that choice, the population will continue to grow and will be ever expanding. Let's apply this understanding to the spiritual lives in the next life.

We know that in this life, if we attain knowledge we then become accountable for our actions. The accountability of gaining education generally leads to the use of practicing that acquired knowledge in some form of career. If we graduate from the University of Life and find ourselves looking for employment in Heaven, what type of jobs would you imagine would be available for the graduates of this earthly existence? Well, considering God's nature of being ever expanding, and realizing the number of children that He has created spiritually, and then given a temporal existence, I would anticipate we will likely have something to do with God's purpose. The Source has a sole purpose to bring to pass the immortality and eternal life of mankind. If He is ever expanding with no limitations, then the experience we received on this earth should have something to do with creation as well. If we are going to become like our Supreme Source, we are likely to continue creating like He has. This is why learning how to create things that are good is not only important in this life, but is essentially requisite for our progression in an eternal realm. Let's suppose our Source assigns the job of expanding His creations. If we were originally created from God's entity, then we could now take the part of us that is intelligence and create other spiritual children to continue this ever expansion of God himself. In other galaxies, there could be a new development of a solar system, including the creation of planets. Everything that we learn here will be of use in the next life. Every experience we have in this life is important to our growth and development to progress into the next life. The very character that we become has been developed by a precise storyline that has assisted us to be everything that God desires us to be. This is why we must be certain that our lives are predicated upon an eternal destiny. Every choice that you make is important, however, every occurance that happens in your life is not necessarily a result of your choice. You are merely an actor, playing out your role in someone else's drama while living and learning to make choices in your own.

I realize that growing up in a dysfunctional home left me with permanent scars, challenges and disadvantages. In many ways, the experience fell short in offering me the basis of what I needed to know in order to learn the essentials of life. I have also learned that had I not experienced the childhood that I did, I could not be on this unique path of life nor could I have had all the experiences that have occurred to date. I would not have the knowledge that I now possess when it comes to understanding children who have grown up in a divorced home. This book is designed to assist in the understanding of the meaning of life and how breaking up the family unit affects the learning curve as well as the life that follows. With divorce so prevalent in our society today, I have a deep desire to ensure that people acquire greater understanding of all that I have outlined. The process of writing this book has also helped me find the purpose to my life through the things that I have experienced and have come to know. This knowledge has become sweeter because of the things that I have come to understand which are in support to our purpose. Now you may think that we do not have a choice in our lives if God controls our destiny, but I will say this much. We come to this life to play a part in other people's drama to help them learn and grow. We make choices that facilitate this learning sometimes to a good or bad outcome. Because God has an eternal view of life, He can change the story so that any choice can be for our benefit. We know that all things that our Creator designs are good and that all experiences we have in life- both good and bad – are for our good. All I know is that this loving Source has helped me to come to know these things and that if you will learn from my story about being a child of divorce, I promise you that God will bless your lives to attain greater things than I have experienced. My main goal is to help you out of the darkness of low energy. This is what is generated in children that grow up in dysfunctional, broken homes where the original creation of the family unit has been destroyed because of destruction or misunderstanding regarding the steps to a healthy creation. Life is always better when we have truth. And truth is found in the light which dispels darkness.

Chapter 11: How Do We Obtain Knowledge?

Dear Children,

Our minds are very complex and acquire information throughout our lives. Everything that our sensory organs experience is translated as information and our brain processes this into short or long term memory to recall at a later time. All experiences, both good and bad are beneficial so we rely on the understanding that results to make decisions and choices. It is likely that without any experience, there is a danger of making wrong choices. In this case, I have found individuals who were much older than me, who shared knowledge that became a valuable tool for the choices that I have made in my life. When someone shared information that I knew contained truth and I applied it in my life, I benefited from it greatly. Unfortunately, I must warn you that there will also be many people in your life that will try to share untruths with you. It will be important to understand how to discern between truth and untruth. In many cases, there will be people who share nothing at all - most likely because even after years of living, they may not be certain themselves about what is important in life and what is not. My intention is to convey the process that I went through to gain knowledge and how I differentiated between what was truth and what was not. In addition, the process revealed to me what was important in my life and what I should use on a regular basis.

We are always learning from the time we are born to the time that we die. We never really stop obtaining information regardless of whether it is good or bad. The experiences that we gain offer us knowledge when they contain truth that will assist in our individual lives. Life is somewhat of a puzzle where the absolute truth or a fullness of knowledge is only obtained when the puzzle has been completed and we can see the entire picture or "big picture" as some people like to describe it. There are a vast number of fragmented pieces out in the world that we have at our disposal to examine, fit together, or discard, as we so desire. The key to obtaining knowledge lies in wanting to know the truth about life and its purpose. Wanting to know is what I would call the motivating force behind our progression. The rate of obtaining knowledge is what will in turn define what quantity of knowledge each person will attain. There is one specific pathway to the end truth. Let me explain this by an analogy of solving a picture puzzle. You can begin at any part of the puzzle in your attempt to put it all together. One strategy I have used is to first flip all the pieces so the image on each piece is visible and I could then identify particular patterns within the scene. The first patterns I would look for are the pieces that have the straight edges on them and particularly, the pieces that have two straight edges because I know that this piece would define a corner of a two dimensional puzzle. Next, I would try to separate the pieces based on their color or image. I would group these together also. So just like a puzzle, we need to develop a strategy to begin our journey of obtaining knowledge or putting the big picture together. This is a very difficult thing to do unless you have some maturity or years of experience behind you. So what did come first, the chicken or the egg? I believe the chicken came first and as with the family, the parents preceded the children. I can only keep stressing the importance that parents must appreciate within their role of developing a strategy for their children. We talked extensively about providing a good healthy environment for children and the overall effects that come upon children of divorce, but let's consider both sides of the coin. In other words, how does the parent play a key role in the child obtaining knowledge, as well as how the child plays a key role in developing their own strategy to obtain knowledge.

The developing fetus, from the time that it begins forming its sensory organs, receives information from the external environment in the form of energy. This energy offers the unborn child both positive or negative feedback and can ultimately either weaken or strengthen the individual. This is why I have emphasized so intensely about providing a good environment for the newborn from the time it begins its initial cellular division to the time when the child becomes an adult and initiates complete independence. Children are like sponges around water. And seeing these sponges soak up information was one of the wonderful aspects of my brief teaching career. I taught elementary school and I can assure you, if you don't like answering questions, then you definitely shouldn't be an elementary teacher. Asking questions is a fundamental requirement to obtaining knowledge and as they say, "There really are no stupid questions". Without ever asking questions, we will never be motivated to seek out the truths of life. There is no time in our lives when we are insistently hungry for information than as infants, toddlers and young children. But somehow we become crippled when we reach the age when our peers are more important to us, and we feel embarrassed by our curiosity for life. So at some point we develop an inward struggle to continue to learn. We face a dilemma when we want to put up our hand to ask a question, and we are struck by the thought of 'being stupid for asking'. I think it is primarily related to our purpose for being here. If we developed a soul conscious mind with an understanding that we are to obtain knowledge through our mortal existence, and carry this with us to the next life, we wouldn't have the reservations developed through body consciousness.

Body consciousness - specifically the ego – will trap you into the limited thinking that is defined by how big your house is, what kind of clothes you wear, how much money you have, what our status in society is, what your job is and most of all, what you look like and is probably closely associated to what you act like. When we live a body conscious life it's not cool to ask questions because we might appear to our peers like we are not knowledgeable and somehow lacking. So in many ways, we are our own worst enemy when it comes to gaining knowledge. When we are afraid to ask questions, and because fear is an ego based emotion, we are in direct opposition to Intention. If God's intention is ever expanding, then the process of obtaining knowledge is in direct correlation with His plan. When we do anything to interrupt that process or His plan, we are in a mode that contradicts our Supreme Creator's intention for us. So all in all, we need to strive for an attitude of learning and being receptive all of our lives. As I was pursuing my education degree, it became clear to me that learning is a progressive process and one that we are meant to embrace throughout life. Elementary and secondary education gives you the basic tools to continue learning throughout your life. Whether a person formally enters post-secondary education or not, there is always a requirement for on-going upgrading of academic skills and life skills. Like no other time in the history of mankind, information is now available and accessible to virtually everyone. Why wouldn't we see this then as an opportunity to advance our knowledge and our capabilities in thinking and learning about truth just as the puzzle-solver must look at the individual pieces and gather information on each, in order to begin assembling the puzzle. We too must create a learning experience in the world that we live, to gather enough information in order to begin putting the picture together. For me, the information was on opposite ends of the scale and only through examining the boundaries did I find where many of the points of truth had intersected. It was a process in gathering information to then be afforded enough knowledge to put the puzzle together.

I grew up on a farm that was very limited to any outside influence of technology and industry. As a child, I learned about working hard on the farm and an appreciation for plants and animals as this was the main industry related to farming. My father was not very focused on helping me learn about the world but more concerned with putting the crops in and taking them off for another year. I'm not sure exactly how I passed anything in elementary or junior high, because there was never any time or motivation for academics within our household. Playing hockey was more important that reading a book so consequently, I never attempted to read anything until I reached high school. Without learned skills to succeed or any motivation in understanding the value of education, I dropped out in grade ten - my first year of high school. In hindsight I shouldn't really be surprised that I didn't finish my secondary school experience. There is a requirement and responsibility on the part of each parent to assist their child to develop a learning strategy for academics and life. If the parent is not showing the child the way or has not done it themselves, then how will the child ever have the ability? It's a characteristic that must be fostered within the developing years of the child. It is clear that without some direction in life to develop initial skills and interests, the young adult will have little or no motivation for furthering their knowledge. I began working in the electrical wholesale industry as soon as I left high school. I stuck at it for five years and learned some basic electrical concepts, but more importantly about talking to other people. I was a very shy introverted person for most of my life to that point. Somehow I got promoted from a shipper/receiver position to inside sales and then eventually to outside sales where I was required to communicate to business owners. This part of my life opened up my character and allowed me to communicate and start verbalizing my thoughts and asking questions. To a certain extent, up until that time I had not allowed my growth and ability to flourish by obtaining knowledge. I remained sheltered and somewhat fearful of all that I did not know.

I was 21 years of age when my father passed away. I was devastated. I had never asked the question before, but now I couldn't stop thinking about what happens to us after this life is over. This questioning led me to a life altering event that changed the course of my life forever.

In April, 1981 I accepted Christianity into my life and entered the world of religion. I had always believed as a basic-fact that God existed, but because I had not received any formal training, I had not committed myself to any specific religion. My father had us baptized into the Protestant faith but we never practiced the religion in the context of our daily lives. We didn't even attend church on a regular basis. I'm not really certain why my brothers and I were baptized. I suspect that people of that era believed they would go to Hell or some fire pit, if they didn't receive this saving ordinance according to Christianity and so they extended this 'seal of salvation' to their children as well.

So at the somewhat tender age of 21, I jumped in with both feet and became an active Christian. Much of my enthusiasm at the time was largely due to the influence of my step-sister. She had been a devout Christian for many years and was encouraging for me to do the same. Embracing the church was an enormous change compared to the dysfunctional home that I had grown up in. The void that I had felt for most of my life due to an absent family was recovered through the fellowship efforts of the congregational members. I was vulnerable to influence. I was doing a lot of soul searching with regards to my existence and just happened to be in the right place at the right time or the wrong place at the wrong time however you want to look at it. I have come to view religion quite differently now from when I was 21. But the experience offered me growth and knowledge and I will always have a feeling of gratitude in my heart for the many things that it had taught me at that time. I have come to know that every experience in life should be looked at as a great blessing from God. Some people believe that their choices have delivered them either happiness or sorrow based on whether they made the right choices on the matter. I have come to appreciate that if something happened in my life it was beneficial for my mortal existence because all things that happen to us are for our good. There is nothing that happens in our lives that is not beneficial for our growth and understanding. This is achieved through God's infinite wisdom and deep knowledge. Coupled with His ability to see the outcome of all circumstances and have each one turn into a learning event for each person. For 23 years I lived the life of a Christian and within that time served a voluntary mission, taught Sunday school and gave of myself in many other capacities. I was married within the framework of religion and had children early in my marriage. Overall, I see religion as a very good institution, no matter what religion, for establishing a healthy moral code and developing values in life. I see religion also as an instrumental tool for raising children and teaching them good principles. It offers a firm foundation to build from, particularly when it comes to understanding our existence in this mortality. It was after this same 23 years however, that I realized that my motivation for becoming a Christian was not of a genuine nature. Religion filled a large void in my life and gave me the family that I never had but my ego was still controlling my life. My enthusiasm and devotion stemmed from my insecurities and I ran to religion to save me. I didn't realize that a real conviction to spirituality would require much more than just receiving baptism and attending weekly meetings. I became a career Christian and fell into the trap of going through the motions of membership. I did not come to truly realize exactly what it would take to come to know God and to lose my life rather than to seek after my life as Jesus taught. What would it really take to know God? It says in the Bible that we must give away all of our sins to know the Lord. When I finally gave up everything I was seeking in the sense of body consciousness and stopped living within the vices of anger, greed, lust, ego and attachment, I came to know the true existence and meaning for being here. Even within the parameters of being a Christian, I still hadn't learned the concept of being acceptable before God. I sought out an engineering and then biochemistry degree just to be acceptable, believing that if I just got some education, I would be acceptable to my peers at church and thus worthy to enter the kingdom of God. And after all that I had achieved, I came to know that we are acceptable to the Lord in whatever form we take and however many achievements or failures we have in our lives. It was only then that I began to fully understand the difference between spirituality and religion. You see, religion is the vehicle that helped me to start asking questions, just as attending university was instrumental in initiating some questioning and acquiring of knowledge. All of the books that I have read since university also helped me to start asking questions. It was through looking at all the disciplines in my life like engineering or biochemistry, that an understanding started to appear. Whether it is comparing Christianity with Buddism, Judaism, or Hinduism, I started to see recurring truths indicating a theme of truth that proves itself much like a universal law. It was through these comparisons that I came to learn that all people in life are on a spiritual path which allows them to evolve over time. I came to see the important role that all religions play in helping move God's efforts along. Spirituality is quite different than religion and knowing the difference between the two can assist you on your own quest in life to make meaning of this mortal existence.

Part 3:
Application
Engineering of
Spiritualism

Chapter 12: Religion vs. Spirituality

Dear Children,

When I sat down to write this book I had two purposes in mind. First, realizing that because your lives had been influenced by divorce, I wanted to share with you my life and struggles, to understand how the effects of divorce kept perpetuating through the next generation to affect your lives. Through this understanding I was hopeful that you would have the tools to end the cycle of divorce and the devastating effects it has had on our family through several generations. The second thing was to articulate the damage that a broken home has on the soul and that the only method of reparation is through a spiritual healing and a complete understanding of God; intended for me to share with you. Soul searching can become distorted by religious denominational differences, and we can become confused in our efforts and thereby miss the mark of our objective. Divorce damages the soul. So the question should not be which religion is correct, so much as, what process must I endeavor to repair my soul from these effects. This is why I differentiate between religion and spirituality. In many ways, if it was not for organized religion, I would not have made it to this point of understanding in my life. So please do not see my criticism of religion as a negative reflection. The advancement that came to me through religion at the age of 21 when my father passed away, helped me to embark on a course of learning that would assist in my healing from these devastating effects of childhood. This initial association to religion, specifically Christianity, led me to study other sects of Christianity as well as other faiths like Judaism, Islam, Buddhism, Shintoism and Hinduism. I also read several books that explained spirituality and the basis of deep meditation in order to make contact with a Higher Power. There were many differences in doctrine and philosophy, but there were also connection points that seemed to ring true to eternal principles or laws that applied to whatever religion I was investigating. I observed truth as it was manifested in my formal education of engineering and biochemistry, by beginning to see a world and universe created by a Supreme Power. And this Creator could bring my soul to happiness by merely searching for meaning. There are different levels of understanding when it comes to deity. It is not my intention to offend other religions with opposing views, but to pull out the commonalities and levels of understanding so that we may see the basis of spirituality within all religions. There is only one truth, which concludes that there is only one God and rather than debate on which religion can offer the most truth, I would like to expand on this truth and how it applies to overcoming the effects of a broken marriage.

In every religion that I have studied, there is a recurring theme of one central figure posed as a Creator. This Supreme Being, appears to be at the core of our beginnings and daily lives while in this earthly existence. This omnipotent presence we have come to call a variety of names such as Supreme Soul, God, Divine One, Baba, Abba, Elohim, Higher Power and Intention, but the underlying commonality with each is that they have had some involvement in our creation. This Creator brought us into this mortal existence for many reasons. The main point is the commonality of this character within each of the religions existent on the earth today. The other theme that seems to ring common to all religions is our spiritual entity. Aside from our purpose for this mortal existence, there is a universal belief that all beings have a soul internal to their physical or temporal body that is considered separate and distinct. Another common concept seems to be based on a mortal manifestation of God. Through a divine messenger whether considered to be a prophet or savior, guidance is offered to the earthly inhabitants. These individuals, whether it is Abraham, Jesus, Mohammad, Buddha or Krishna all have teachings that result in bringing the world population closer in harmony with the one Supreme Being. Anything beyond this tends to get everyone confused about their purpose for being in the world. There have been countless wars and fighting over beliefs and possessions based on philosophies regarding which interpretation is more correct. I don't believe that a loving God or Creator would allow for such variation without purpose. Suffice to say that each religion is very important for the evolution of human consciousness. Whether someone is Jewish, Catholic, Buddhist, Muslim or Hindu, each soul that comes into this life will have a vehicle or means for becoming acquainted with God and defining a specific pathway for life. The important point here is the word "pathway" and recognizing the significance of following some precise faith that will lead you to further light and knowledge. By becoming acquainted with different religions I have grown to respect each dogma and method to purify the soul in order to lead the spiritual being through this mortal existence.

It has been described that life is an adventure and what would be the adventure without some type of roadmap. Religion forms a basis for structure in learning about life. It allows us to have common association with fellow believers and gives us the opportunity to be in harmony with other souls that have come to experience earth. We are able to find intimate companionship to initiate marital relations, which will eventually produce offspring necessary for sustaining life on earth. Within the infrastructure of religion we are able to learn about our existence and essence of being. We can learn how to teach our children about life, and allow them to be associated with good moral values that produce high energy experiences. Through religion we can see the interconnection that we have with others souls and to respect their existence and the role that our lives play through these interactions. Religion allows us to be of service to our community and to be receptive to needs of others. Religion however, should not be a means of isolation or separation from other souls in the world. This is where religion begins to become muddied in its effort to unite all souls in the world. If everyone was to take several steps back to the basis for our existence and purpose, that we are all souls, that we all have a common Creator, and that life is a drama of events allowing us to interact and grow as a result of these interactions, we could go a long way to eliminate prejudisms. Humankind has come far in this regard over time. There is greater acceptance as a result of becoming more of a multicultural society. Most of us have come to learn respect for differences – cultural, lifestyle, religious, color of skin or otherwise. But the affects of divorce have caused us to face other challenges represented by the alter-ego. While religious beliefs in general have opposed the destruction of the sacred unit called family, most have now abandoned this foundational platform to accommodate its prevalence in society. It seems that even religions have become defiled by divorce and has created an acceptance of this plague within the walls of their own institutions. This plague needs to be battled not in the differences of doctrine or multitude of philosophies regarding which religion is correct. It needs to be addressed on the basis of the fundamental beliefs of soul consciousness. It is the fundamental lack of love and regard – within a defined family unit - that affects the development as a human being.

In the beginning, when we came to earth, there was a separation from God. Our memory was voided regarding this separation as we were brought into a family union. We were whole within this family. Our pre-mortal existence was based on the parentage of God, and in His loving wisdom, he allowed us to enter mortality into another family unit headed by parents. The separation with God was not unpleasant because we immediately entered a familiar setting in our new family existence. However, because of our fallabilities, divorce entered into the family union leaving the immortal soul with a feeling of disconnection from the original association. Once again, because of the lack of love and regard, vices developed as a survival mechanism over separation. Human beings became very ego driven and individuals were defined by who they appeared to be. I am a Christian, or I am a Jew or I am Muslim. The separation from God and lack of a supporting foundation in life created a total body conscious experience that manifested differences and beliefs based on a lack of true understanding. This is what religion has come to. If we distance ourselves from body consciousness and consider soul consciousness, we would come to understand and see each individual as living souls created by a common Supreme Spirit. Humans, in their separation from God, began to reach out for our Divine Creator.

Through my many and varied life experiences I have learned about something that will bring you closer to your Creator. Have commonalities with close friends and associates that share in your belief of God – it will bring you closer to Him. Let religion be a vehicle within your lives, to find truth and happiness. Ensure that you are associating with people who are in search of similar truths but do not get caught up in the routine apathy as people sometimes get pigeonholed into one form of thinking. God's mind is ever expanding therefore your mind should also be ever expanding to accept new knowledge as you are prepared for it. As I mentioned before, human consciousness is an evolutionary process. My hope is that each generation will understand a little bit more and make a further progression to overcome the effects of divorce. Through this understanding you will learn how to identify with your spiritual center to bypass the characteristics developed from separation. You can then go on to develop healthy relationships that may evolve into long term loving partnerships. Such strong unified associations may be supportive as a basis for the family unit. Religion is one of the vehicles for you to find the truths you require to becoming a healthy soul. Having achieved a full and deep understanding will allow you to acquire peace and enlightenment in this life and in the life to come.

Chapter 13: Understanding True Principles

Dear Children,

An important means of attaining peace and happiness in your life will be by subscribing to true eternal principles. In other words - embracing truths that coincide with God's nature. You will come to understand your nature by understanding the nature of the Divine Spirit as you are the very essence of His being. Life is like a pathway that each person walks along to discover self and the character of who they are. When we understand truth or true principles, we understand ourselves because we were created by the Supreme Soul who is the author of truth and must also abide by true principles. Truth is like light. Untruth is darkness. Darkness can be made light but light cannot be made dark. When light exists, darkness cannot, therefore, when we know truth, untruth will cease to exist. Part of the purpose of life is to differentiate between what is true and what is not true. Much like a scientific experiment, a hypothesis can be developed for truth. If we perform an experiment upon truth, we will gather results of the specific truth that was tested. From the results we can understand what is true and what is not true. As a human being, we have a variety of ways to experience truth which is generally associated with our sensory system. Through seeing, hearing, touching, smelling and tasting, our mind gathers information to make sense of the world we live in. Dr. Hawkins has indicated that all things that our sensory can experience have some type of energy association. He and his team have measured various elements using kinesiology in determining whether something can either strengthen or weaken the human soul. Within his map of human consciousness we can learn how different sensory can be defined as either negative or positive contributors. Through experimentation on occurrences in life, one can determine if that specific experience is enlightening, relating to being a positive contributor or whether it is filled with darkness, which would be specific to a negative contributor. Life is a laboratory that will provide many events for you to experiment with. You will either be strengthened or weakened by the experience which will allow you to determine if this may add to your understanding of truth. When you see certain results replicating over and over again, you come to understand that this principle can be a proven truth or untruth. In general, if something you are experiencing makes you feel good, peaceful, empowered or strengthened, this can be defined as a truth. On the other hand if an occurrence makes you feel bad, shameful, or uneasy and it weakens you, then it will be clear that this is an untruth. God's nature is all about being good and peaceful, which is the essence of your nature. So when you come into contact with something that makes you experience the characteristic that you were created from, you know that it is telling you that this experience is good and can be attributed to truthfulness. These are the facts that we are striving for. This certainty is the basis of peace and happiness that a successful life can be built upon. When we deviate from truth, we will experience pain, sorrow and unhappiness.

If we go back to understanding the devastating effects of divorce, we can understand that children of various ages are left to feel abandoned, rejected, neglected and without love and regard. This event has been thrust upon them and there has been no consideration for their feelings towards what has been instigated by their mother, father or both parents. The child's natural state is peace - having come from an existence of love with the eternal Supreme Creator, who provided all, particular a unified family of spiritual brothers and sisters. Children are closer and more perceptive to their nature from the recent spiritual union that they enjoyed in the pre-mortal existence. Rather than feeling loved and nurtured through a similar experience, they feel cut off from the unity as they are now engulfed in a family that is filled with disharmony and contention. They feel betrayed by the people who intended them into this life with their creative capabilities. The power of creation is sacred and to be treated with utmost respect. Creating another human being is likely the greatest responsibility that we will ever encounter. So when this child, at whatever age, experiences not only the spiritual separation of mother and father, but also the temporal separation, the child begins to develop vices or survival techniques to replace the love and regard that is lost. These vices include but are not limited to anger, greed, lust, ego, attachment, mistrust, lying, people-pleasing and other forms of addictions that are driven by an ego-based character. Ego is an enemy to God, and that ego is born out of fear. Where fear exists, God cannot. Fear is the antithesis of faith. Separation for a child causes a great deal of fear, combined with the experience of neglect and lack of love and regard are all contributing factors towards the development of a vice-based character. The Hindu belief indicates that each soul that comes to the earth is entitled to love and regard. When these fundamental nurturing elements are absent, a character filled with vices emerge and Maya is born. In Hinduism, Maya and ego are synonymous. The ego also promotes a body-conscious life that dictates identity based on status, appearance, wealth and ownership of material possessions. Given all of this, if finding truth is finding God through ourselves, not only are we placing a huge wedge between ourselves and our Creator, but we are way off the path in aligning ourselves with truth-based principles.

As children grow from infancy to adulthood, they experience development that usually promotes phases from dependency to independency. For obvious reasons a 9 month old baby is more dependent on its mother and father than a five year old, or an eight year old or someone who is ten. The more independent a child has become at the time of divorce, the less long term effects may develop. This may also attribute to the fact that the child has had a longer experience of a unified family before separation occurs. One might argue the fact that the child may not have a complete consciousness of the separation at an early age thus creating a more critical period relevant to awareness, but I am not necessarily convinced that consciousness is only perceived by awareness. Human consciousness is defined by all sensory and to what extent the infant is receiving negative contributors is measurable. So let us take it from the standpoint that the child feels a lack of love and regard because of this separation. The first thing that the newborn experiences is fear. Fear then gives birth to Maya. Because Maya consists of various characteristics, here is an example of what may occur within the child. Anger is probably the first characteristic that the child of divorce experiences after fear. We have a natural tendency for fight or flight in fearful experiences, and it is quite likely a six year old child is not going anywhere in flight, so the natural instinct is to fight back. The child may be observed in acting out, having temper tantrums or having blatant outburst of anger, which will generally have a similar response from the parent. This response by the parent and lack of understanding may cause an emotional repression within the child. The child may also become withdrawn in their verbal communications, which gives growth and nurturing to the ego. The ego says, "Well if your parents won't take care of you, then don't worry, I will take care of you." The ego teaches the child to mistrust, because the parents have lied and caused them a lot of pain. The youngster learns how to lie to avoid the emotional pain or consequences that may occur as a result of telling the truth. The child sees themselves as being different from other children that have parents that are together, such that greed and lust are born because of the desire for what they have lost. The child learns how to people-please in order to get the desired response. The child learns not to trust the drama but becomes controlling in order to get what they desire. I believe this is rooted from children initially feeling responsible for their parent's breakup. Their ego tells them that if they had just been a little bit better as a child or did things a little more perfect, then their parents would have stayed together. Some children of divorce are perfectionists and some are people-pleasers. Both of these tendencies cause a lack of self-respect because they are continually trying to gain acceptance from others. This loss of self-respect will be mirrored externally and they will find companionship with people that do not respect them. Can you imagine a marriage of two people that lack respect for each other and yet they are codependent? Disastrous consequences are assured. Attachment is another characteristic of Maya which disallows healthy personal growth, primarily due to a lack of trust. The ego will try to compensate for the marital shortcomings by putting a higher value on body consciousness. The ego will drive people to define themselves by their achievements such as attaining higher education, to provide an elevated status in society. There is nothing wrong with achieving higher education, as long as you are doing it for the right reasons. If you are doing it for status, then that indicates that you do not understand who you really are as a soul and you are attempting to attain a false sense of security. This same thing is manifested in physical appearance, material wealth and ownership. These body conscious elements are all associated with darkness, or negative contributors. And darkness cannot exist in light. As long as darkness is retained, then light will be denied and our very purpose of being and progression will regress. Light and dark cannot exist together. A child of a broken home, or possibly a dysfunctional home cannot understand the true association rooted in childhood development. Most people rationalize as adults that they have gotten over the effects of their dysfunctional childhood - which they have moved beyond those early days and bear little or no scars from the experience. But without knowledge, light or truth regarding the real effects from childhood, one cannot shed light into the darkened areas that seems to come back automatically under certain circumstances.

Truth and principles of truth came to me in a variety of ways. When I was 21 I was tired of partying and riotous living. When my father passed away, I reflected on my childhood and had a deep desire for a family of my own. I started to think about what kind of family I would have and what kind of a husband and father I would be. I also had thoughts of our existence and where our beginning was formed, and more so, where would our life take us after this life was over? Obviously, my father had just left this existence, leaving me to ponder where he had gone and to what purpose we have here. I continued to consider this event as one of the greatest occurrences in my life because it caused me to start asking questions about our existence, rather than just living naively day after day. I looked to religion as many people do when they feel spiritually weak. I spent 25 years fully embracing Christianity. This religion offered me opportunities to travel to other parts of the world and to learn about diverse cultures. The Bible is the basis for one source of light for learning truth, but Christianity also taught me other disciplines that allowed for post-secondary education which expanded my knowledge in the sciences, humanities and other studies. These educational pursuits expanded my knowledge of belief, philosophies and cultures. I started to realize how ethnocentric we are in North America and how our culture and beliefs have given little room for other religions and understanding. Now that we are becoming a more diverse continent, we have developed a greater respect and understanding to help us see truth in other cultures and walks of life. I was fortunate to leave this continent over 20 years ago to start to make the associations that I have come to respect in life today. I attained truth through relationships within career and personal associations. I found truth in all kinds of books and all religions that I became knowledgeable of. From asking questions of our Supreme Creator over 25 years ago, my mind has expanded to a comprehension that can only be attained through continual searching and listening. I see this life as a scavenger hunt, and have been hunting for its purpose for most of my years upon the earth. One of the most recent questions that I began asking was why I haven't been successful at staying married. This is when I began to understand myself and my purpose for being here on earth. I could never quite understand why God would let me down by sending me to a broken home where pain and sorrow was a common daily emotion. I realize now how my understanding may help my children in this world where divorce is so prevalent. After 13 years of marriages, and four children later, I came upon conclusive answers that I knew would not only be valuable to me and my children, but also to others that have suffered the effects of divorce.

The key to overcoming the effects is obtaining truth and not just any truth. The more truth the better, but the ultimate truth is coming to an understanding of who you really are. Once you do this, you can slay the dragon - or Maya - by learning a new way to live. This new life will burn away the vices and kill the ego. This new life will promote soul consciousness rather than body consciousness. This new life will not be easily obtained because it requires taking the red pill rather than the blue pill. Placing full trust in truth will allow the Matrix of life to become clear and allow you to see the reality about your existence and the very purpose for being here. It is all about understanding the effects of divorce, the birth of Maya or Illusion, and how to destroy that ill-fated belief and replace it with light and an ocean of knowledge. The fact remains that our Supreme Soul or Eternal Parent has woven our lives into a beautiful tapestry of events and each occurrence has been for a reason. Even in the Bible it is recorded that all things are good and are for our benefit, both good and evil. It wasn't until I thought deeply about the Omnipotent Spirit's eternal perspective that I came to believe in the Drama of Life. We are all just actors in each others lives offering meaning and helping each other grow. With God's eternal perspective, events and people could be orchestrated to allow for corrections in our earthly education. Our Creator knows everything eternally in the past, present and future. The Divine knows what we will do and the choices we will make long before we ever make them. So what would prevent a loving parent, who has sent us here for this earthly schooling, the opportunity to write the curriculum for our lives?

Chapter 14: Understanding the Drama

Dear Children,

I've heard many different explanations regarding our mortal experience. Some have said that life is a drama in which our lives go through progressive stages of learning. Others have said that the world is a stage in which we are all actors within this human drama of life. Screenwriters have even suggested that life is a staged event as portrayed in the movie, "The Truman Show". Initially, as children, it is difficult to see this. In my early childhood years I did have a similar inclination towards the possibilities of this truth. Then later, as I progressed with education and the psychological understanding of child development, I become convinced that this was just an egocentric phase that I was going through. So I passed off the idea as somewhat of a humorous thought. In my search for understanding I have come across many different beliefs about the human drama.

In the Christian belief and other Bible-based religions there is an understanding of a Supreme Being, a God who is our loving Creator and Heavenly Father who provides us with an earthly existence for our growth and learning. Many of the Asian religions such as Buddhism, Taoism and others, show respect for wisdom and teach us how to live through moral conduct, much like the Law of Moses in the Bible. There is a respect for ancestors and all human life that contributes to the world and universe. In the Hindu belief there is a basis of rebirths similar to the cycle of rebirth in Asian culture of climbing the ladder of understanding. The Hindu belief suggests a cycle of 5000 years which consists of a Golden, Silver, Copper and Iron Age in which souls come down to the earthly existence to learn and grow. No matter what belief it is, there is always an element within the doctrine which promotes an evolution of understanding. Recently, I made a connection with a meditation center that is closely aligned with the Hindu belief which suggests that individual souls come down to earth from a Soul World, and enter into the 5000 year cycle at some point. Where you enter the drama of life, is highly dependent upon the nature of your soul. Some souls will enter into the drama in the higher Golden Age, while others will enter into the Silver, Copper or the lowest Iron Age. Souls that are more spiritual in nature, or what is known as Brahmins, tend to enter the cycle in the Golden Age. Souls that have a greater tendency for body conscious elements of status, wealth and materialism, will enter the cycle in the Iron Age. The later you enter into the cycle, the less lives you will be reborn into. But regardless of the point at which you enter the drama, you will still gain whatever understanding that the Supreme Soul has sent you to acquire throughout whatever number of births you may have. The last phase of the Iron Age is called the Confluence Age defined as the last birth before the cycle ends and the beginning of another cycle starts with the Golden Age.

In the Hindu belief, it is understood that each soul plays an important role within the drama of life. Much like a written script in a theatrical play, God writes the script of life to ensure that each soul learns to their maximum capacity. When you consider a good movie that you recently viewed, it likely contained an enticing beginning, climactic middle and conclusive ending – hopefully a happy one. In academic studies, we examine distinct parts to the written story, such as the protagonist, the antagonist, the plot, the red herring and so on to the extent that only a good written and properly planned script can produce something that provides an effective experience for the audience. If we as human beings have intelligence, how could we possibly believe that a Supreme Being and loving Parent who created the heavens and earth, does not have a perfect plan for this drama? Just as this earth is perfect, as it orbits around our solar system, we too have perfectly planned lives on this planet to assist us in our growth and development. I have always had trouble understanding this concept because it seems to suggest that life is predestined without any real individual choice in making decisions. But that's not the case at all. Our lives are filled with choices and we are free to make them. Individual choice is very important in our everyday lives as it helps us to mature as souls and develop characteristics similar to our Godly parent. We learn through the choices we make – good and bad. There is no question that the Divine Spirit has a huge advantage over us as mortal beings. Primarily, He is immortal, much like our souls, with the capability of seeing past, present and future all at once. I will expand more completely on how God directs us as our loving parent in the next chapter on "Understanding God", but suffice to say that much like being a parent here in this world, if we are a good parent; we try to ensure that our children learn from their experiences. Sometimes we prevent them from doing things that we know will harm them, because we have "been there, done that". It is natural for a parent to want to protect their offspring from harm. At other times we allow our children to wander a little so they may develop an independence and ability to make their own choices. Ultimately, no decent parent that has any instinct of what's good for their child would let them go astray to the point of being lost completely. If our very nature is suggestive of this fact, then how much more concern will a Supreme Creator have when it comes to directing and guiding each precious soul to its ultimate perfection. At times, we get too caught up in the symantics of life and differences in philosophies that we get confused about which way is the perfect path. The truth is that all paths, no matter what they are, are important in the life of each soul.

The drama is a perfectly planned script that allows us to enjoy a life filled with choices and yet, experience the bliss of having God as our director to guide us back to His presence. Each soul is living the life that it was meant to live and playing a role in the lives of others that they come into contact with, not by some mere coincidence, but by a decided agreement, a sacred contract. There are many important reasons for this scripted drama. First, it helps us to understand that all things that happen in our lives are for our good. That if we rely on our belief that a loving Creator is guiding our existence, life then becomes less burdensome with regards to whether or not I will pass the test of time. There is no one way in God's school and if there were, He would have designed it that way. There are many different people, cultures, beliefs, religions and philosophies – all with worthy purpose. All of the elements of life create the context of a great story, for God loves a great story and is writing the most beautiful creation of all, called "The Drama of Life". Understanding the drama also allows you to be able to differentiate between your soul and your identity in this mortal existence. In soul consciousness, I am not my body, nor my occupation, or appearance, wealth or status in life. This is merely the role that I play on this human platform. Imagine yourself as an actor hired to play the part in a theatrical performance. You are not that character but you are merely a professional actor playing the part in a story. When you arrive at the theatre, you go to your dressing room and prepare yourself with both mind and body to come out on the stage to perform the role which has been selected for you. You then play the part exactly as it is scripted, and then go back to your dressing room, take off your costume and go home for the rest of the day. Similarly, we go through this same procedure every day of our lives. The actor, who lives outside of the theatre, exists in a soul conscious state. Some performers, without the knowledge of the drama, will wear their costume home at night or in other words, they will be fixated to a body conscious state at all times. Some souls will be willing to take the red pill to understand what is real, and some souls will not be willing to partake of this same knowledge, but will be more inclined to stay within the cushioned, safe world they know as the Matrix. There appears to be a correlation between the times that the soul enters the drama, for example in the Golden Age as compared to the Iron Age. Souls living in the Golden Age may have more of a willingness to accept a full understanding of soul consciousness while those who enter in the Iron Age could have a tendency to remain inside the Matrix. It may not be an easy task to accept the drama and acquire full comprehension. Such a task requires accountability. But understanding both soul and body consciousness will allow you to function more effectively in the world and remain detached as an observer, rather than to be convinced that you are the part you are playing. I'm sure that most people would feel quite comfortable playing the part of someone who is very wealthy, has a lot of status in society and is very attractive according to worldly standards. But imagine if you did not meet up to these standards? What if you had all kinds of trials and adversity in your life that left you to be very poor, without material wealth or status and unattractive? There is no differentiation between souls in the world. In fact, in God's eyes, we are all equal. It is only through our own separation from the Supreme Soul, that we cut ourselves off from this soul consciousness to live a life void of this ultimate understanding. If you are acting your part in the drama 24/7 without ever taking your costume off then you are missing the point of who you really are. True life allows you to remove that costume and embrace your divine essence.

The ego-based Maya, with its characteristics of anger, greed, lust and attachment develops in children of divorce as we have discussed but it can also be the outcome of other base dysfunctions. This might include any type of environment that does not promote a feeling of love and regard, where neglect, abuse or addiction prevails. I have focused on divorce because I know how it has affected my life and developed me into an ego based, body conscious individual. The biggest reason that someone is unwilling to take off their costume is because the dysfunctional mortal experience, which was rooted from the early beginnings of their lives, has left them feeling afraid. They have lost touch with who they really are in a soul conscious state because the ego has tried to convince them otherwise - and often has done a very good job of it. The parental responsibility that was lacking in their life left this soul abandoned, confused and rejected. They developed mistrust, uncertainty and fear. These characteristics gave birth to the ego that taught them to lie, deceive, flatter and people-please. They used these tools to acquire a false sense of security by obtaining a body conscious state of materialism, wealth, status and vanity. A soul living in this state of consciousness cannot take off their costume because they don't know who they really are. As long as the ego and body consciousness fuels the false sense of identity, the individual will have no motivation to search deep within themselves to find the real person, the true soul. Let's be honest with ourselves, if you have material security in this life, for example a million dollar home in a posh neighborhood, a job as a professional with lots of status, you drive a Porsche, have a million dollars in the bank and look like a beautiful model, would you really be concerned about who your soul is? Perhaps not, but then again, you might be searching for a higher meaning more than the beggar who is on the street corner. After all, money does not buy you happiness. And there is no greater joy to be had than to know yourself. People that have spent their lives attaining material wealth, status and possessions of the world often have been sucked into the Matrix and they can't get out without understanding. And comprehension is only achieved through soul consciousness. A similar story is played out in the life of Jesus when he beckons the rich young ruler to sell everything he has to follow him. Now this wealthy individual was not a bad person, in fact it outlines in the scriptures that he had done everything else required in the law. Jesus knew however that the greatest challenge would be for the wealthy ruler to relinquish his kingdom and trust that a better world would be offered to him. Jesus understood that all of us would be challenged with this concept in this mortal life. To overcome the body conscious state of materialism, wealth and status and trust in the Divine Creator who promises us ultimate freedom through a deeper understanding of truth. Life is a drama with a continuous series of acts. Within each act we are reborn again and again until our progressive perfection as God would have us, is complete.

I am not a believer in reincarnation in its traditional sense. I do believe that we are reborn many times in a lifetime of many levels of human consciousness. Like the souls who come down at different parts of the drama and live a distinctive number of lives, each soul that lives in a mortal sense will experience new beginnings at different cross-roads of life. Every time we learn something new or have an experience that brings us closer to our true nature, we are reborn to another level of human consciousness. Life is similar to the seasons that pass by each year. In the spring the buds beginning to develop on an otherwise dormant plant; the grass begins to grow and babies are introduced on wobbly legs learning to take their first steps. I grew up on a farm and remember the beauty of a new born calf taking its first steps. There is life, excitement and fresh rain to wash off the dust and nourish the new life. Once full grown the life enjoys the beauty of the summer months. The heat from the sun rays beam down to ripen the crops in the fields to a golden brown. In the fall, the leaves begin to turn, offering an outstanding array of colors that will eventually flutter to the ground with the advancing force of the cooler winds. The trees will then become barren, not dead, only sleeping, resting until the next season of growth.

Our lives follow a similar pattern to the seasons. Knowledge comes to us as a spark of light, a feeling of hope, and thought that motivates new beginnings and knowledge. The newly obtained awareness then sprouts into a living organism that requires nurturing and nourishment for its growth and development. Good knowledge will produce good actions and secure peace. Alternately, bad knowledge will fall on the same ground attempting to prevent or reduce the growth of a good plant. One must weed out that bad plant in order to promote continued growth of understanding. The heat of the sun will ripen the plants that have become strengthened through good knowledge to the point where one is ready to harvest that plant. As the farmer combines in the fall, one must store up that knowledge which has been produced for it is the product in one's life. The winter winds blow as the snow accumulates on the ground. The whiteness of the snow reminds me of wisdom that is churned from knowledge. As the harvest is stored in the bins, knowledge over time will become wisdom that will grace the life of the soul in its eternal pursuit. The soul will reap the rewards of wisdom through searching to find its real self. As you come to know your soul, you will be able to understand the meaning of the drama. You will understand your role and the part that you play in the lives of those people whom you meet. When you find your real self, you will also find all the virtues of God, the Supreme Soul from whom you are derived. When you come to self-realization, you then come to know the Supreme Soul. You will be able to make better choices in life, because you will understand who you are and what you need. You will understand your purpose in life and thereby attain a greater level of satisfaction and personal achievement. You will gain greater self-respect and radiate that respect in an attraction for an equally self-respecting companion. You will understand your role as a parent and the responsibility you have to your children from the very beginning.

I have come to understand why the drama was the way it was in my life. Where I used to resent and regret, now I am thankful for the knowledge that came to me as a result of the life I lived and continue to live. My life has become meaningful in a time of disparity. It has helped me to see how much I have to offer spiritually, when I have very little materially. The drama has helped me to see how my part as an actor will not only shape my life but also the lives of those that I associate with. If it wasn't for the life I lived, I wouldn't be writing these words for my children to share with them for their profit and learning. Life is evolutionary and each generation helps the next to attain a greater level of understanding. If all I accomplish in this life is to help my children to be successful, have understanding in the sense of soul consciousness, then I will have completed the most important task I could possibly ever endeavor. My task has been to first help them understand that they are a soul, second that they were created by the Supreme Soul, our Creator and Heavenly Parent and last, that the drama of life is accurate and is proceeding exactly as it should. This drama of our life is the most beautiful story ever written by a loving Godly parent that has an ever-lasting concern for our well being while we partake in this University of Life. When you understand God, you understand yourself and when you understand yourself, you understand all of life and everything in it.

Chapter 15:
Understanding God

Dear Children,

I remember when I was about six years old my mother taught me a prayer for blessing the food. It went, "God is great, God is good, let us thank Him for our food, Amen". God is great and God is good. At six years of age, I did not fully understand the power of this phrase but I have since come to appreciate that everything that is good is God. To understand our Divine Creator, is to understand what is good. Our Heavenly Father is a being of beauty, kindness, love, creativity, unlimited abundance, ever expanding and receptivity. These are characteristics I find more frequently as I become increasingly aware of my existence as this temporal creation. It makes sense that if we are God's spiritual children, the root essence of who the Spirit Soul is, is also within us. As we discover the virtues that are innate within ourselves, we then come to know the God that created us. Anthea Church, in her book, *"Inner Beauty, A Book of Virtues"*, has defined thirty different virtues and used beautiful words to describe them encouraging the reader to identify with each characteristic. Some virtues are on the surface, and others may be hidden deep within the heart that has become clouded by the deceptions of ego. Virtues are described as high energy or positive attractors, a constructive power that can help us identify with our Creative Parent. Dr. Hawkins has so eloquently developed a logarithmic scale for this concept that one can begin to see the power of consciousness starting at neutrality around a log of 250, and then ascending to enlightenment at a maximum log of 1000. Therefore, not only can we identify with God and His characteristics of being, but we can also become empowered by identifying the virtues that exist within each human creation. Our ability to recognize these virtues has been covered by a multitude of lies that the ego has manifested through its association with what the Hindu belief call Maya or illusion. Dr. Hawkins indicates that the mean operant of society seems to be around a log of 207, which is just slightly above the consciousness level of 200; that associates to courage. In his map of human consciousness, courage is the lowest energy virtue and everything below it, I would consider a non-virtue, as indicated in pride, anger, desire, fear, grief, apathy, guilt and shame. The base virtue that all human beings begin to identify with the existence of God is courage. This relates to being an adult child of divorce, in which the main reason we lose consciousness with our internal soul is from the development of ego which is born out of fear, from separation, abandonment and rejection. Thus, the antithesis of fear is courage, and it is courage that allows for the beginnings of identifying with the soul. Empowerment will create a basis for searching within ourselves and having courage to remove the layers of illusion to determine who we really are. Through this process, each individual can begin to understand who God truly is. By staying within this positive consciousness, it is possible to attract other virtuous experiences that will continue to elevate the mind to come to a greater comprehension of God. These experiences can come through various sensory such as thinking, activity, speech, visual, audio, smell and touch. All positive attractor experiences will provide constructive power and elevate the level of human consciousness. This enlightened state will correlate to virtues that reflect the characteristics of God. As an individual begins to feel the virtues within themselves they become part of the real self, they begin to experience an understanding of God and His essence of being.

God is our Creator. In the literal sense we are referring to the existence that we live. We know that from a Biblical account, He created the heavens and earth. He created our mortal bodies to initiate mankind and our reproductive expansion that would populate the earth over thousands of years. Creativity is a root for many other activities and occupations. We create literature, buildings, thoughts, food, jobs and any other possible thing imaginable. In essence, everything in our existence has been or will be created. The world's population continues to expand. Our knowledge of technology and science continues to grow. Our capabilities as humans and our concern for our environment and resources continue to enlarge as well. The reason that God creates is in order to expand and continue His influence throughout time and space. Astronomers and scientists have developed telescopes and space shuttles to explore the frontiers of space. But there is still very little understanding or just how far space exists. I asked a good friend what He thought about God and His existence. He told me that He believed we were to God, as are microorganisms are to us. Can you imagine our whole universe could possibly be contained within the space of a tiny micro-organism? Our Divine Creator would know of our existence, but we would have a very limited capability to experience His. Yet, we understand from ecosystems that each organism is vitally important for the existence of another. We don't really know the extent of God's influence and existence however; we do know that we must play an important role in His effort to expand His influence throughout eternity as infinity has no beginning and no ending. The Supreme Spirit's creations will be never ending, simply because there is never an end to anything. As we learn how to create, and there has to be a proviso that the creation is in alignment with God, who is good, our creations and influence will assist God in His ability to expand into eternity. So in order to create good things, we must first be healed of our inabilities that get in the way of this expansive power that has been entrusted to us, God's children. This is the reason for understanding why healthy relationships between two people need to be the basis of healthy future creations. And the central and most important creation of all is a child that has just been newly formed, with a pre-existent spirit dwelling inside and ready to begin life and to develop into a healthy human being that will also be able to create good in the world. Through the divorce process, this delicate foundation is distorted and broken to the point where the individual is not aware why they cannot create good. They cannot comprehend why they continue to have problems in their life. It is because their creative wand has been bent and broken – it will require repair, through understanding, before they can go forward and fulfill their task of creativity and goodness.

The next area of understanding is that God is our spiritual parent. He has given us the opportunity to be parents in this mortal life and it carries a tremendous responsibility for the growth and development of another human being. When I saw the effects of my first divorce I initially passed them off as just another experience that had failed and that I would need to keep moving forward to be successful in the next relationship. It wasn't until after my second marriage, and many failed relationships after, that I started to realize something had gone terribly wrong in my life that needed correction. This was the basis for entering therapy and revisiting my childhood to understand how it was affecting the choices that I was making as an adult. I began to comprehend that no divorce is a good divorce. The only opportunity to minimize the damage would be to address the effects that take hold of little children at this important time of development and how they have been disrupted by these traumatic events. I started searching for material that would assist either parents of children or adults who had once experienced divorce and were now having problems in their relationships. The first book I found that offered assistance to parents was entitled, ***"Helping Your Kids Cope with Divorce, the Sandcastles Way"***, written by M. Gary Neuman with Patricia Romanowski. The second book was entitled, *"Adult Children of Divorce, How to Overcome the Legacy of Your Parent's Breakup, and Enjoy Love, Trust and Intimacy"*, written by Jeffrey Zimmerman. I was astounded how very little information there is on the topic of being an adult child of divorce. There is so little that has been written on the effects of separation and anything that would help a person overcome the dysfunctions. Here we have a society plagued with divorce that is ever increasing, where now 1 in 2 marriages fail. Likely the majority of our problems with juvenile delinquency, crime, immorality and the destruction of values in society, likely come from people who have experience a shattered childhood. And yet, very little emphasis is put on understanding what is at the root of this problem and how it may be cured. Our society just seems to be developing more systems to deal with the problem. There are simply more lawyers, more court rooms, more psychologists, more jails, and more legal counsel - when there is really no one addressing how to cure the problem. Of course, one way of ensuring the root of the problem is dealt with is to ensure that couples never divorce. But this goes against the free will and choice of a society, so we know that is not going to happen. The more practical approach is to help individuals understand who they really are, and the value that they hold as a creation of the Divine Spirit. And in understanding how precious we are, we will respect and uphold each other and value our relationships more and be less inclined to divorce. For we will understand that a broken home has tragic consequences for our children and ourselves, and we will pour more energy and understanding into making relationships work rather than tossing in the towel. God has empowered us to create children and He would want us to act responsibly by being good parents to the children that we have created. And parenting requires two parents. Yes, there are unfortunate circumstances in life that cause the family to lose one of the parents, however, generally speaking, our mandate as a couple should be to the child we have brought into this world. Every child was, in most cases, created by two loving souls and they are counting on two healthy parents to continue the journey as a supportive family unit. Parents that have brought a child into the world have an obligation to stay together so that the child can have a healthy upbringing that will allow them to develop into an empowered human being free from the effects of an unhealthy ego that will do nothing but harm them for the rest of their life. If we know that it requires two parents to make a child, I am going to make the assumption that God expects those same two parents to also raise that child. Being a parent is the most challenging experience that I have ever had. But it has also been one of the most rewarding and has taught me two essential characteristics -giving and receiving.

First let's look at the concept of receiving. Stephen R. Covey said in his book, *"**Seven Habits of Highly Effective People**"*, seek first to understand, then to be understood. If we are to first understand, this would imply that part of our character must be receptive. To receive information means we must listen, observe, smell, taste and experience - all associated to a particular set of requirements for parenting. In general, we receive information through all aspects of sensory and for the most part we try to learn to receive only input that is constructive and positive in nature. This type of information will add power and strengthen our capabilities in life. We try to be objective in our thinking and constructive with the information when it is received. When our children are toddlers, parents are required to taste and touch all things that may go into their mouths to ensure the safety of the child. We observe the actions of the child on every level that may require our guidance. Not only are we visually observing the child, we are also active listeners in understanding the needs of the children that we have created. We use the smell sensory to know when it is time for a diaper change or possibly when to speak to our teenager about the use and addictions of nicotine and marijuana. Receiving is an important factor as it is the basis for our response. The quality of our response will depend entirely on the accuracy of interpreting the information that was initially received - this is why seeking first to understand, then be understood is so important. If all we ever do is to be understood, then we are only responding on the basis of our own consciousness without a full input from the participating party. When I trained as a teacher, I learned that it is important to test for comprehension. This is no different when you are communicating; trying to appreciate the level of consciousness or interest someone may have for a specific topic. The method to test comprehension is to ask questions, which is either required to initiate conversation with teenage children or to direct the conversation with younger children. With a spouse, I have found asking the right question is the key to seeking first to understand. However, all in all, when parenting or interacting in the world, receiving information is a critical factor to be successful, therefore we must get good at asking the right questions.

The next basic skill that God encourages us to learn is how to give. I saw a young man walking across the pedestrian cross walk in front of my car the other week, and his T-shirt said, "Taker". This caused me to reflect on something a friend of mine told me once about everyone in society. My friend explained that in this world there are Givers and Takers. The Givers tend to be more selfless and able to offer in a compassionate sense, things to others, while Takers have learned to selfishly exploit the resources of others to satisfy their own needs. The child of divorce has developed an ego through the vices of Maya and has an inherent trait for lust, greed and attachment. Because the child was never given what it needed and deprived of the love and regard through separation, the ego taught the child to want that which it could not have. The ego taught desire for body consciousness – including materialism, wealth, praise and appearance. In many ways advertising has exploited this weakness in society to promote a craving for vanity, sex and lust. These are all characteristics of the unhealthy Taker. On the other hand, there are the Givers. The healthy development of a child will display the antithesis of lust, which is love. The concept of love is rooted in giving selflessly in an unconditional manner to anyone for whatever cause or circumstance. This type of love is first exhibited within the family and is portrayed through the healthy relationship between a father and mother. Through the act of parenting, one also learns the act of love with the natural affections that are felt as you experience your bonded child's life and interact within it. The rate of marriage and commitment to have children is declining in the developed world, and this reality is combined with the increased rate of divorce and lack of role models in the life of developing children, so is there any question why we are creating a world of Takers rather than Givers?

There is a specific reason that marriage is a sacred bond and union between two people. It is the training ground for developing love, trust, kindness and all other virtues associated to happiness. It says in the scriptures that, "Men are that they might have joy", and one of the ways of receiving joy is to truly understand who our Creator is so that in turn we can understand ourselves. When we are one mind, heart and strength with God we can then accomplish anything that we wish to do. We are empowered with this knowledge which frees us from the ego-based entrapment that limits us in an eternal realm. This is the training ground for understanding God, so unless we get to the bottom of who we really are, we will never come to that understanding. We will merely exist on the basis of our ego and live with a limited knowledge of our existence in this life. Eighty years is only a blink of an eye in an eternal life. I hope that this book may have helped you understand why divorce is so restrictive to limit our understanding and even our motivation to understand. I know that since coming to this knowledge my priorities have changed. I have come to focus more clearly in seeking a deeper understanding of God and of my purpose in life. I know that as we come to understand the Supreme Soul, we will begin to understand life. It is not until that moment that we will be prepared to meet our Creator and live in His existence as a family as we did prior to coming to earth.

Chapter 16:
Understanding Life

Dear Children,

Life is like a pathway, we can take many different routes and we will learn something from whatever passage we take. God has an eternal perspective and can give us the experience we need for whichever pathway we have chosen. You might ask why there are so many religions. Why such a variety of cultures that support different philosophies of life? Why so many different jobs or even status levels in society? Life and our understanding of it, is evolutionary. When I think of what I used to believe in and what I used to understand about my life and purpose for being in this existence, it has changed completely over time. In my early years I thought my life would always be the same – and I had no reason to think otherwise. But things did change and true reality was revealed to me as I decided to take the red pill. At each level of understanding, the drama and our ability to interact with those in our circle of influence, expands. We make the choice, God then provides the actors in our lives to teach us the things we need to understand in order to evolve. Caroline Myss also describes this in her book, *"**Sacred Contracts**"*, the non-coincidental associations that occur between the individuals that we interact with in life. God is a perfectly planned Supreme Being that does not allow for accidental experience. You can see the structure and organization of His universe and yet how could we believe that His most precious creation, humankind, formed after His very likeness, is left to some coincidental mishap. Caroline Myss suggests that the relationships we had in our premortal existence were the basis of how our relationships would develop in life and that the people who are very close to us, such as our immediate family members, have all agreed to play some important role in our lives in order that we may evolve our understanding.

I have started to wonder why some people have good experiences and why some people have bad experiences, why some people have riches and the luxuries of life, while others are poor and wonder each day how they will survive with what little food they have to eat. The ego teaches that you are your body, therefore, if you are poor then you are worthless, if you have no material wealth, then you have not been wise in life, if you are unattractive and do not dress like a supermodel, then you will not be praised or envied by others. These are the disadvantages of living in a body conscious state. When you live in a soul conscious state, you understand that each soul, whether rich or poor, has great value because you recognize every soul as being a child of God, a soul that was created from the essence of the Supreme Soul. Each person in life merely plays a role that will provide for the experience of another. When we look at life in this manner we can apply greater wisdom by using less judgment upon others and ourselves. How does that saying go? "We are our own worst critic." Until we understand the workings of the ego and how it manipulates our lives, we can never break free of its vices and enjoy true peace and happiness.

Life is meant to be filled with joy. For each of us at birth there is a mixture of circumstances so we begin at different pathways on the road to happiness. Some will start their lives in good religious homes rooted in ethical and moral teachings that will offer a solid start for the newly arrived soul. There will also be souls that begin life in war-torn countries where freedom of choice may be minimized by a ruthless dictatorship. There may be souls who are born in countries with very little resources and poverty abounds, forcing people to make life and death choices each day on just how to survive and obtain food for their families. And still other souls who enter in very prosperous parts of the world but are imprisoned by the abuse of dysfunctional families. So many variations of where each soul can begin their journey, yet we all have the common initiation of being souls that have come from a pre-existence. If we look at each other in a temporal sense, we are divided by our differences which have caused wars, struggle for power and inflict great sorrow and pain. If we see each other in a spiritual sense, then we are unified in our commonality as we share the same Creator. The key to life is getting back to this spiritual understanding. Each pathway will provide distinct challenges for each individual, but as knowledge is acquired, and wisdom is obtained through using good judgement, we can come to understand the meaning of life, and the purpose for our existence. Good judgement comes from making good choices. Life has no guarantees regarding the outcome of choices that we make. There are times when we think we are making a correct choice but then later realize, from the sorrow that was experienced, that an alternate choice may have created more happiness. There are also choices that we make that only involve ourselves as well as choices that involve another soul. One of the greatest decisions that we can make is who we will offer a commitment of marriage or partnership to. This is a choice that has to be considered with a great amount of reflection and meditation. Time needs to be given to understand if the relationship has a natural flow of existence. Because decision making is critical, one must determine the compatibility of the other with regards to making choices together and having unified thoughts. One thing you can be reassured in is that God will not leave you helpless in all these choices that need to be made. As earthly parents know when to allow for more individuality or when more direction is required, God will also know when to allow us independence and when to be more directive in our lives. Understand that all things are for our good. Whatever choices we make, the consequence may vary, but our Creator has an eternal view of events and His intention is to help each soul benefit to their greatest capability with every experience they have. God's intention is to assist each soul to identify within them the very godlike creation that they are and once they have come to this understanding, each soul's choices will be in complete harmony with God's mind. It says in the Bible that

God the Father and Jesus were of one mind, one heart and one strength. This was the ultimate message from the Savior of the world. To choose spiritual over temporal, God over ego, happiness over sorrow, virtue over vices, soul consciousness over body consciousness and so on. Some choices are easier to make than others, but choice is always the basis of whether we receive happiness or sadness in our lives.

Maya or illusion in the world will try to persuade us to make more ego or temporal based choices rather than Godly or spiritual based. Temporal based choices will provide for limited happiness but more likely sorrow will follow because this type of happiness cannot be sustained for a long period of time. Whereas spiritual based choices will give unlimited happiness. My ego based decision motivates me to buy a brand new BMW or Mercedes Benz convertible because this will make me feel successful and validate who I am, from a body conscious state of mind. But the truth is, after some limited amount of time has passed, I come to the realization that my new car functions with bells and whistles, operates no differently than a brand new Ford Focus. I am able to get from point A to point B with the same efficiency and the same amount of time (legally) however, there is quite a substantial difference in the amount I have indebted myself. It may become sorrow at a later time by the financial burden I have brought upon myself. We have broken this concept down into the basis of needs and wants but advertising has exploited our egos and made wants and needs clouded in our decision making process. A simple and revealing question we should always ask ourselves is, "With this choice, what type of circumstance am I CREATING?" Remember that one of the fundamental lessons that our Supreme Creator has sent us here to do is to create only good things. If we foresee anything bad that may come from a creative choice, we are only asking for trouble and bringing lessons of sorrow upon ourselves. So if you remember only one thing from this book remember, "ONLY CREATE GOOD THINGS IN THIS WORLD. GOD WILL CORRECT YOUR BAD CREATIONS OVER TIME BUT ONLY AFTER YOU HAVE PAID THE PRICE OF SORROW FOR YOUR MISTAKES."

The key to life is to understand the laws that govern this world and all of the universe and eternity. We know of some basic laws that we have just come to accept as a part of our existence. One such law is the Law of Gravity. This law predicts that a force is exerting itself downward toward the earth. We know that this law cannot be defied until we travel into space. If you throw a ball up in the air, it will return downward with the force of gravity acting upon it. Scientists have even been so accurate as to measure the acceleration that an object will fall with gravity acting upon it. We also understand a more spiritual law called the Law of the Harvest that teaches "we reap what we sow". Much like a farmer that plants his seed and watches it grow into a crop that he may harvest - the actions, thoughts and words that we have planted in the world will come back to us in the quality and quantity that we initially offered. This is also known as karma by the Hindu belief that identifies much of our sorrows with actions that a soul has performed in previous lives. I recently read a book in which the author very eloquently tells a story of a sage who is living along a mountainside. The sage teaches a visitor some of these laws of life. Dan Millman, in his book entitled, *"Laws of Spirit"*, captures the truth of laws and brings to the forefront, laws that we cannot ignore. I would encourage any seeker of truth to read this revealing work. Much like the law of gravity, when we understand the laws and learn how to implement them into our lives, we can reap the benefit of their understanding. Understanding spiritual laws will not only make us wise but will also provide experiences in life that we can add to our success portfolio. When we learn eternal truths, we can better understand the laws that our Creator abides by, and thus can bring us eternal happiness not only in this life but also in the life to come. This is what investing in an unlimited future is. We will come to understand what really matters in this life for our futures in the next life and what does not really have any eternal worth. Remember, that we come to this earth alone and are merely given a mortal body to house the spirit of our existence. We then leave this mortal existence, leaving everything behind excluding our spiritual form and the knowledge that we obtained from our mortal experience. Even the relationships that were formed here, we had already developed in our pre-existent world. This should help you to understand that only the soul conscious knowledge will have any worth in the life to come. I am not saying that you do not need the temporal life to assist you in your journey while here on earth, but emphasizing that you need to evaluate just how important your temporal things are, and with what magnitude are you being distracted from your soul conscious effort of connecting with the Divine

Spirit? All that God wants us to do is to place our emphasis on spirituality more than temporality. As we live out our lives in the drama, playing the role that we do, our first and foremost thought should be that we are first souls and second, we need to recognize that we are to create only good, and remember God at all times. If we create good, then we must be one with the Source and how do we do that if we do not remember our Omnipotent Creator constantly every minute, and every second in our lives? We must seek truth by receiving information through our sensory receptors, and have a choice between high and low energy that will either strengthen or weaken us. We must distinguish between what will add to or take away from our quest for spiritual truth. Lastly we need to respect other souls who are also on this journey through mortal existence. There will be souls in the drama that will play a significant role in your life and learning, and many others will merely pass you by with only a smile, never to be seen again. Life is a drama, a beautiful story of each soul's mortality that assists them to become all that they can be. When we stand back, it is a tapestry of woven threads that display a magnificent array of color and pattern that only a God, our Immortal Heavenly Father, could weave.

Chapter 17: Putting It All Together

Dear Children,

I was watching the movie, "Paycheck" the other night, and I noted one of the lines that was used. The character said, "… When you can see the future, you take away hope." There is truth in this. If we could see where we were going after this life, we would have no need to hope because our knowledge would be perfect. For this same reason God erased our memories of the life that we had in our pre-existent form. One of life's purposes is to gain faith and faith is preceded by hope. With faith we know that miracles occur, the blind are healed, the deaf are made to hear and the disabled to walk. To a certain degree, we have all experienced miracles in our lives. The key to seeing them is to understand that they do exist. If you do not believe in miracles, one could happen right in front of your eyes and you wouldn't recognize it. I have had so many miracles happen in my life, that I have come to understand the truth of the things that I have written in this book. This book in fact was a miracle and was accomplished as a result of many events and miracles that contributed to gaining this understanding that I am sharing now. When I came to this life, it was not in the most desired setting. I have come to understand the damaging effects of being a child of divorce. Instead of offering you riches, wealth, status, fame and material acquisitions, I offer you the wisdom that I have acquired over the past 52 years. So let's start from the beginning once more and put it all together.

You, like I, were created by a loving God in a pre-existence, long before the creation of the world. We were created by a matter called intelligence from the very essence of the Source. Your creation was called a soul and took on a form in the appearance of your temporal body. This intelligence has the form of a very high energy similar to the electrons that orbit around a nucleus of an atom. Your spirit, like these electrons shares a commonality with all energy, including God, and all the elements that are known on the chemical periodic table. Your energy or spirit is the same and one with the Divine Source and all other electrons that exist in the world. If you took away all nuclei of everything that existed, and the electrons in spiritual form were light, then all you would see is one bright light. There would be no difference in each spiritual creation. We would all be one and the same. This is an important consideration when seeing other temporal beings. Recognize that they are you and you are them, we are all one. When we were created temporally, we separated from God in a spiritual sense, but our purpose in life is to understand that we are always connected to our Source as we were created from Him. And we are also connected to all other temporal creations, because we share the same Source. We came from a family of spiritual brothers and sisters. God created a similar existence to come to and begin our mortal journey. Souls come to the earth at different times because each specific soul benefits from the particular time that they have come to the earth. I have asked myself many times why I came at this point on the earthly timeline. Suffice to say that the world evolved to a point that it was ready for each soul's arrival and that each soul would contribute in a significant way for the drama to progress. It is helpful to parallel this thought with the Hindu belief of the cycle consisting of the Golden, Silver, Copper and Iron Ages. Souls that come to the cycle in the Golden age live a more spiritual based consciousness. The spiritual consciousness then slowly declines to a temporal or body conscious existence, with its last life concluding in the Iron Age, which includes the Confluence age. This is the last life before entering the new cycle of the Golden age. Souls that enter the cycle in the Iron Age will focus more on their temporal being, and the world in general will be focused on body consciousness. These conditions can be observed in the world today. Each soul however, has an important role to play in the drama and comes to earth at just the right moment to be able to play the part they have chosen with their Creator to optimize their learning experience. It is reassuring to know that each life that is created has a specific plan. The Divine Source has outlined and has scripted the perfect play to help every soul learn all that is necessary in this life.

Each soul comes to a different experience as well, whether a country or culture they are born in, the socio-economic status they encounter, and what religion or belief system they have adopted. Over the last 50 years, the structure of the family has been disrupted significantly in comparison to its original form that was initiated thousands of years ago. The format for children to be conceived was only made possible through co-union of a man and women, and was generally consentually agreed upon by both parties. For the most part, the man was the bread winner while the women's responsibility was to rear the children at home ensuring for their proper needs and nurturing. Only in the last 50 years has this format changed and we are now seeing families with less children due to economic constraint, usually double income earning professionals that generally leave the child rearing responsibilities to some other form of authority and we see an ever-increasing number of broken homes due to divorce. Neglect and abandonment of children due to improper economic circumstances, broken homes due to infidelity, spousal and child abuse – these issues have never been on an increase in any point of history more than they are today. Souls that are born in today's world are faced with extraordinary challenges and devastating long term effects. Until these root issues are addressed with individuals that have been exposed to divorce and its deleterious consequences, society will continue to experience an ever increasing destruction of the family unit. These broken homes will continue to produce children who then become adults incapable of having healthy, loving, long-term relationships without the understanding to heal.

In a healthy relationship, where two parents are concerned about their child's well being and development, you will see sacrifice on the part of the parents. The parent is a teacher, concerned about the child's experience and what they will absorb through their sensory system. Parents attempt to make sure that the child receives high energy input – similar to their pre-mortal experience and conditions. The child will inadvertently make wrong choices and will be exposed to low energy experiences that will help them differentiate the desired from the undesired. Parents will ensure that the child feels a great deal of love and regard to avoid the potential for Maya or the ego developing the vices of anger, greed, lust and attachment. These parents will also assist the child to relate to their more spiritual side and characteristics through formal religious devotion or some form of spirituality regarding surrounding creations. A spiritual community will be important not only to the child, but also to the parents who are seeking to stay spiritually minded, avoiding low energy experiences and growing interdependently and as a couple on a spiritual plane. The child's interaction with the parents during the early years of development will be intensive and the time will be well invested when the child begins to reflect and make decisions to associate with high energy experiences. Simply put, the parents need to portray an example of virtue both inside and outside of the family unit. As vices and body consciousness are allowed to creep into the family, such influence can be devastating if it is not eradicated. Overall, today's society is experiencing body consciousness that contaminates the family and its values, and this is driving households to live beyond their economic means and capabilities, increasing personal debt and bankruptcy. This focus on money and materialism is causing society to become greedy as they lust after material wealth, and temporal acquisitions. As the focus of the family becomes more ego driven, the soul consciousness fades away just set aside for some rainy day. Children who grow up and have a positive experience with both parents are able to use this fundamental information to form their own relationships on the basis of attracting high energy contributors. If this process is deviated in any way, leaving the child without love and regard, abandoned or rejected, then these healthy characteristics will be overtaken by the unhealthy ego. It's as if the ego says to the child, "OK, so if your parents aren't going to teach you how to survive, then leave it up to me to show you." In divorce, the child will develop an unhealthy ego as a result of abandonment, rejection and neglect. The more that parents can reduce the fear of separation, and ensure the child can have a life filled with both parents, the more capable the child will feel to deal with this at a later time. I maintain however, that no divorce is a good divorce and I advocate parents staying together and working things out for the sake of the child.

A wise parent who had many years of experience in social work told me that when two people get together, they are entirely free to decide whether or not they would like to continue the relationship on the basis of its current success. However, once the decision has been made to have a child, there is no longer an option for ending the marriage because of the absolute necessity for co-parenting the child. Unfortunately, our society has not shared the same view, and now we are seeing the long term devastating effects of these self-satisfying decisions. Children need both parents to develop into healthy human beings. These parents need to be operating under the same roof and not attempting to use some 21st century philosophy to pad their mistakes. When parents begin to see that they are creating children who are incapable of having healthy relationships perhaps they will start thinking more about the child than about themselves. If the married couple are experiencing problems related to being an adult children of divorce and do not have children, it is best that they wait to have a family until the childhood divorce issues are resolved and there is a complete understanding and commitment on both parties that they will work through these matters to avoid a future divorce.

Now that we are in the thick of the plague, let us address what people need to recognize about themselves to heal before entering into a relationship, and also, for people who are now in an unhealthy relationship, what they can do to heal themselves, to avoid inflicting the consequences of a divorce upon the children of the marriage.

A healthy mind and spirit is marked by gaining knowledge and being empowered. Whatever stage of life you are in, your starting point begins with healing yourself and recognizing that divorce has rendered you with some inherent characteristics that have weakened your ability to have a healthy relationship. This inability is not only with other individuals but also with you. Difficulties in developing healthy relationships include not only personal relationships but also business interactions. If you are currently in a personal relationship, it is imperative for you to share this healing information with your partner to have their complete understanding and support -particularly if they have not experienced life as a child growing up in a divorced home. In some cases, even adults with similar broken home histories will not understand why they feel the way they do and act as they do. Realize that because you have been neglected of love and regard as a child, you have developed ego based characteristics that may include anger, greed, lust and attachment. You may view your life and existence from a body conscious state, valuing yourself on the basis of status, wealth, materialism and appearance. You likely have also learned to manipulate and try to control outcomes by lying, cheating, people-pleasing in attempts to get the desired response. The ego is an entity that has been born out of fear of separation, and has become completely alienated from the soul, God and any soul conscious thought. People that have gravitated to religion but have failed to recognize the ill, self-serving effects of an ego are in essence only followers of the religion by word and not by action. Jesus himself said that there will be many that come to him to profess that they know him. Because of their vain efforts as a Christian, He will tell them that He never knew them. It's like the old saying, "Don't just talk the talk, but walk the talk." Realize that until the ego is destroyed, and all its other inherent characteristics, you will still be functioning under these ego-based survival skills learned in childhood. As we mature, we may learn to overcome these by having healthy input through our companion, friends and associates. It's important to understand that your nature may be to revert back to the old ways of dealing with a situation when you feel threatened. There will likely be an automatic association of fear and ego which is activated in the fight or flight scenarios within the confines of conflict. For healthy people that can deal with conflict, disagreements are seen as a normal element of relationships. To adult children of divorce, particularly in high conflict divorce, conflict induces fear and raises many red flags.

As adult children of divorce, you must realize that one of the first steps to healing is to acknowledge that you are no longer a child and that you can take control of your current situation in relationships. Your clarity in understanding this is crucial in order for you to respond in an appropriate manner. If possible, the person in your conflict also needs to be aware of the old ways in which you dealt with conflict. It is important for the non-adult child to act appropriately, to minimize the escalation of conflict and also ensure that either person is not threatened with abandonment, rejection or neglect. The cold shoulder, silent treatment or threatening to divorce is extremely frightening to the adult child of divorce. If any circumstances of the conflict seem to parallel conditions that the adult child of divorce experienced in childhood, such as yelling, uncontrolled screaming, physical or verbal abuse, the adult child of divorce will quickly revert back to childhood consciousness in an attempt to defend themselves. A couple experiencing conflict must do everything possible to keep discussions objective rather than taking any personal hits or body blows. Adult children of divorce tend to do as their role models did in their lives - following the same example of improper fighting. One must recognize however, how much more significant this is to an adult child of divorce than someone who has not experienced divorce in their lives.

Success for an individual will depend on how effective they have healed themselves of the ego. Whatever means you have to take in order to become more soul conscious will allow you to let go of the ego/body consciousness. Soul consciousness may be obtained through religion and many spiritual philosophies available. I have implemented raja yoga meditation with a combination of daily readings and church attendance to meet my spiritual needs. The mere recognition of your intrinsic value as a spiritual child of God will help you detach yourself from being valued in a material world of money, appearance and possessions. Once your knowledge of existence changes, you begin to see yourself in a much different light. In the Hindu religion, it is believed that through yoga meditation, Karma is burned away or in other words, Maya ego-based characteristics and body consciousness begins to dissipate. The illusion of Maya becomes apparent and one can begin to see through the Matrix of life. In the Christian faith, belief in Christ and repentance of past sins will eliminate former mistakes. The key in all of this is recognizing what the real sin is for adult children of divorce. What was once viewed as a sin was merely a means to survive. As we become more soul conscious and less body conscious, striving to eliminate the vices to obtain the virtues of truth and light, adult children of divorce can go on to live happy lives filled with peace and harmony. It is important to be healed of the deleterious effects in order to have a healthy self image. If adult children of divorce portray an image of self disrespect, chances are they will attract other individuals who do not respect them as well. They may be initially attracted to you because of their own deficient needs but over time their disrespect will manifest in your marriage, should it get to that point, and you will find it very difficult to work through issues. The compounding effect of being a child of divorce, struggling with inadequacies, with a partner who has no respect for you in the first place, is almost too much to bear – and there most certainly will be a breaking point.

A relationship is something that is developed over time. Adult children of divorce tend to either avoid relationships altogether, or they rush into the relationship, to gain immediate intimacy and feel a sense of love and regard. Either way, it's not a healthy approach for such an important union and life changing event. We as children of a Supreme Soul are here to learn how to create good things. One of the most important things that you will create is a union with a life long partner. At some point you may decide to create children as well. Such decisions need to be made slowly, with much contemplation. I recommend getting to know many people over a long period of time. Over time you will gravitate to some by having more in common with them. This should be a social endeavor to understand the many different types of people there are in the world along with their values and beliefs. As you are more attracted to someone, do not lose yourself in immediate indulgence. Take lots of time to get to know them, even if they seem to be a potential life long partner. I recommend getting to know someone for at least two years in a courtship scenario before even considering talking about marriage. If the relationship naturally progresses into a strong union, this relationship must mature for at least another three years before even considering having children. This is only a minimum length of time to get to know someone, before a marriage commitment and then to have children – you can certainly take longer. Remember, that all creations that we make if good in nature, will last a very long time and continue to bless our lives. Anything that is miscreated, that has a significant life changing association, can create grief and sorrow that may haunt you for the rest of your life. Be very aware of conditions that have occurred in your life, some of which you had control of and some you did not.

The effects of divorce - a choice that your parents made, has likely affected you in many ways that prohibit you from having a healthy relationship and to make good choices. But if you understand this, and make a concerted effort to change the early years of damage, you can heal from these effects before going on in your lives. The principles that I have learned can be applied at any point. The sooner that you learn these things and apply them in your life, the sooner you will obtain sure happiness and inner peace.

As they say at the Meditation Center, "Om Shanti" - translation: "I am a peaceful soul." May you have continual peace and happiness – a treasure that is greater than any riches in the world. It is my hope that through understanding, divorce will never be part of your vocabulary or any part of yours or your children's lives ever.

Life will not be perfect but the drama is accurate and all things happen for a reason. Many times we cannot understand why bad things happen to good people but know that we have a loving Creator who ensures that all events that we go through will benefit us in our mortal experience. Know that there are many spiritual truths for you to learn and understand in this life. Even if I told you all that I know of, it would not impact your life in the same manner as you discovering these things for yourself. Be conscious of the truths that exist to bring you happiness. Much is gained by understanding and as we begin to think like our Supreme Creator, we will gain many of the attributes and virtues that are present in God. As you believe in the Source and soul consciousness, there is no need for ego because you realize that you are made from God. There is an inherent value that cannot be defined by any worldly measure. As you live in soul consciousness, you will develop a faith so powerful that it will be capable of overcoming any fear produced by the ego. You will learn that following truth will also help you develop faith to overcome any fear or uncertainty of this life or of the life to come in eternity.

Conclusion

Dear Children,

I realize that we have walked a long hard road. At times I have felt weary bearing the burden of understanding how being an adult child of divorce has affected me, but I also know that through soul consciousness, life can change overnight. One does not have to be a silent sufferer of the effect of this modern day social dysfunction. It is merely a matter of deciding to gain the knowledge of understanding, making changes in the way you respond in relationships and ensuring that each and every day is lived to its fullest. And as you live, you can be thankful for the drama and each opportunity that you have had to learn and experience this life. Remember that when you change the way you think about something, the thing you are thinking about changes. And we all need a bit of a paradigm shift in our lives from time to time.

Material things will only give you a moment of pleasure, but understanding who you are from an eternal sense will offer you a joy that money cannot buy. Always do your very best and live the kind of life that you would imagine that God lives, for He does live in each of us every day as we come to recognize who we really are, "Children of God".

Book Credits

Judith Wallerstein, "The Unexpected Legacy of Divorce"
Wayne Dyer, "The Power of Intention"
David Hawkins, "Power vs Force"
Caroline Myss, "Sacred Contracts"
J.K. Rowling, "Harry Potter"
Stephen R. Covey, "Seven Habits of Highly Effective People"
Anthea Church, "A Book of Virtues"
M. Gary Neuman; Patricia Romanowski ,"Helping Your Kids
Cope With Divorce, The Sandcastles Way"
Jeffrey Zimmerman, "Adult Children of Divorce; How to
Overcome the Legacy of Your Parent's Breakup and Enjoy Love,
Trust and Intimacy"
Dan Millman, "Laws of Spirit"

MOVIE CREDITS

Laurence & Andrew Wachowski, "The Matrix"
M. Night Shyamalan, "The Village"
Andrew Niccol, "The Truman Show"
Philip K.Dick, "Paycheck"

Manufactured by Amazon.ca
Bolton, ON

38921798R00127